WITNESS MISIDENTIFICATION IN CRIMINAL TRIALS

WITNESS MISIDENTIFICATION IN CRIMINAL TRIALS

REFORMING IDENTIFICATION PROCEDURES TO PROTECT THE INNOCENT

Aaron Spolin

Library of Congress Catalog Card No. 2019919901

ISBN 9-7816717876-6-7

Spolin Law P.C.
11500 W. Olympic Blvd., Suite 400
Los Angeles, CA 90064

Table of Contents

Chapter 1

INTRODUCTION

On a night in the beginning of July 1984, Jennifer Thompson was raped. While the rape occurred, Ms. Thompson studied her assailant so that she would be able to later identify him. Ms. Thompson ultimately identified Ronald Cotton as her rapist and was absolutely certain that Mr. Cotton was the perpetrator. "Several days later, looking at a series of police photos, I identified my attacker. I knew this was the man. I was completely confident. I was sure. I picked the same man in a lineup. Again, I was sure. I knew it. I had picked the right guy, and he was going to go to jail. If there was the possibility of a death sentence, I wanted him to die. I wanted to flip the switch."[1] At trial, Mr. Cotton was found guilty and sentenced to life in prison. The case was later retried, and this time Mr. Cotton was found guilty of *two* rapes and sentenced again to life in prison.

Prior to the second trial, an inmate named Bobby Poole had bragged about committing the rape. When he was brought to the second trial, Ms. Thompson looked at Mr. Poole and testified, "'I have never seen him in my life. I have no idea who he is."

In late 1994, Mr. Cotton's new attorney filed a motion for DNA testing, and in 1995, the DNA results showed that Mr. Cotton had *not* raped Ms. Thompson. In fact, Mr. Poole had raped her. Mr. Cotton, an innocent man, spent almost eleven years in prison because a witness was absolutely certain that she had seen him when, in fact, she had not.[2]

---

[1] Thompson, Jennifer. "I Was Certain, but I Was Wrong." *New York Times*, https://www.nytimes.com/2000/06/18/opinion/i-was-certain-but-i-was-wrong.html, June 18, 2000, accessed on August 8, 2019. The facts of this case come from Ms. Thompson's op-ed and the National Registry of Exonerations, https://www.law.umich.edu/special/exoneration/Pages/casedetail.aspx?caseid=3124, accessed on August 8, 2019.

[2] Mr. Cotton and Ms. Thompson-Cannino co-authored a book about their experiences, *Picking Cotton: Our Memoir of Injustice and Redemption*, New York: St. Martin's Press, 2009.

Among all the shortfalls of the criminal justice system, none is as pervasive, institutionalized, and dangerous as the potential for eyewitness misidentification. Accidental misidentifications are not only the leading cause of faulty convictions but also the cause of more faulty convictions than all other causes combined.[3] Indeed, many legal scholars and misidentification experts believe that mistaken eyewitness identifications are "conceivably the greatest single threat to the achievement of our ideal that no innocent man shall be punished."[4] This widespread danger exists because of the underlying psychological conditions of human memory, the extensive use of police procedures that exacerbate the problem, and Supreme Court case law that institutionalizes a scientifically incorrect understanding of this danger.

Judges and lawmakers have known about the general frailties of human memory—and their potential for injustice—for thousands of years. Ancient Jewish courts, recognizing the dangers of eyewitness accuracy, set an incredibly high bar for any witness willing to testify against a suspect in a capital case.[5] A conviction required the direct observation of the crime by two witnesses, strict rules for the nullification of contradictory testimonies, and numerous other safeguards and stringencies limiting the potential for a wrongful

---

[3] Koosed, Margery Malkin. "The Proposed Innocence Protection Act Won't—Unless It Also Curbs Mistaken Eyewitness Identifications." Ohio State Law Journal, 2002, 279; Wells, Gary L. "Eyewitness Identification Evidence: Science and Reform." *The Champion*, National Association of Criminal Defense Lawyers, April 2005, 12.

[4] McGowan, Carl. "Constitutional Interpretation and Criminal Identification." William and Mary Law Review, vol. 12, 1970, 238.

[5] Himelstein, Shmuel, Rabbi, trans. *Mishnah*. Maor Wallach Press, 1994. Vol. XI, Sanhedrin, Chapter 5, Mishnahs 1–2 (discussing the merits of an examiner who would question witnesses regarding minute details in order to assess their accuracy); Polish, Dan. "Capital Punishment on Trial: Does Judaism Condone Capital Punishment?" *The Workmen's Circle*. https://circle.org/jsource/capital-punishment-on-trial-does-judaism-condone-capital-punishment-by-rabbi-dan-polish/, accessed on December 23, 2019.

conviction.[6] Moreover, a witness who contributed to a wrongful conviction by testifying falsely on a capital case was put to death.[7]

Needless to say, the standards for witness testimony have come a long way since their use in ancient Jewish courts. Nonetheless, in the modern United States criminal justice system, there are very few set rules governing how witness identifications are to be elicited and when they should be allowed at trial. The result is a system that allows misidentifications to bring about faulty convictions.[8]

While the criminal justice system gives defendants a host of protections at trial, many of these protections are useless against procedures that effectively condemn a defendant before the trial has even begun. As Supreme Court Justice Brennan noted in *United States v. Wade*:

> The trial which might determine the accused's fate may well not be that in the courtroom but that at the pretrial confrontation, with the State aligned against the accused, the witness the sole jury, and the accused unprotected against the overreaching, intentional or unintentional, and with little or no effective appeal from the judgment there rendered by the witness—"that's the man."[9]

As a result of this potential for what is effectively a pre-trial conviction, lawyers, judges, and the courts have recognized what Justice Blackmun described as the "inherently suspect qualities of eyewitness

---

[6] Himelstein, Shmuel, Rabbi, trans. Vol. XI, Sanhedrin, Chapter 5, Mishnahs 2—4; Maimonides, Moses. *Mishneh Torah*, Edut, Chapter 4.

[7] Himelstein, Shmuel, Rabbi, trans. Vol. XII, Makkot, Chapter 1, Mishnah 4; Nagel, Yehoshua. Personal Interview. December 22, 2019 (explaining the meaning of the term *zomemim*, referring to false witnesses).

[8] TerBeek, Calvin. "A Call for Precedential Heads: Why the Supreme Court's Eyewitness Identification Jurisprudence is Anachronistic and Out-of-Step with the Empirical Reality." Law and Psychology Review, Spring 2007, 21.

[9] *United States v. Wade*, 388 U.S. 218, 235–236 (1967).

identification evidence."[10] Eyewitness identifications, as Justice Brennan concluded, are "proverbially untrustworthy."[11]

Incorrect eyewitness identifications play an enormous role in all types of faulty convictions and pose a particular danger in death penalty investigations when the stakes are high for both the defendant and the police department anxious to solve a heinous crime.[12] Among all crimes—capital and non-capital cases—eyewitness misidentifications account for more faulty convictions than all other causes.[13] Specifically, eyewitness misidentification accounts for one half to two thirds of these mistaken convictions.[14] The rate of known eyewitness misidentification is about as high in capital cases, which is particularly troubling given the fact that "victims make up the vast majority of eyewitnesses, and live victims are rare in most homicide cases."[15] Despite this rarity, eyewitnesses are the leading cause—by far—in faulty death penalty convictions.[16]

Studies of wrongly convicted capital defendants place the error rate based on eyewitnesses at 50–75 percent.[17] The Innocence Project at Cardozo School of Law found that, among those freed from death row through DNA exoneration, 75 percent were convicted in cases of "mistaken eyewitness identification."[18] A similar study by Ayre Rattner, a professor of sociology, found that eyewitness misidentification was the direct cause of 52 percent of wrongful capital

---

[10] TerBeek, Calvin. 34.

[11] Ibid. 38.

[12] Of 365 inmates who were exonerated based on new DNA evidence, 69 percent had been convicted based on "eyewitness misidentification." Innocence Project, accessed on August 7, 2019.

[13] Wells, Gary L. "Eyewitness Identification: Systemic Reforms." Wisconsin Law Review, 2006, 615.

[14] Clements, Noah. "Flipping a Coin: A Solution for the Inherent Unreliability of Eyewitness Identification Testimony." Indiana Law Review, 2007, 275.

[15] Clements, Noah. 289.

[16] Koosed, Margery Malkin. 275.

[17] Ibid. 279; Wells, Gary L. "Eyewitness Identification Evidence: Science and Reform." 12.

[18] Wells, Gary L. "Eyewitness Identification Evidence: Science and Reform." 12.

convictions.[19] Moreover, a prominent study on witness misidentification, which will be discussed below, suggests that the rate of misidentification has risen since several prosecution-friendly Supreme Court cases in the 1970s.[20] In short, the problem is clear, pervasive, and—as will be shown—exacerbated by current investigative and legal standards.

Throughout this book, I will examine the current misidentification problem and suggest a number of unique policy changes. First, an overview of police eyewitness procedures will provide some orientation as to what is occurring in modern police departments. Following this, I will examine the underlying psychological data that show how inherent flaws in human memory create a risk for misidentification that is far higher than one would expect. The next section will explore how police procedures exacerbate this problem with "suggestive" practices that often fail to sufficiently test witness memory. While the academic discussion of misidentification usually ends here, I will go on to discuss two areas that are often ignored by the literature: the vastly underestimated dangers of cross-racial identification and procedure in place that withholds from jurors the tools they need to evaluate identification accuracy. After this and before delving into reforms, I will discuss how Supreme Court and lower court case law has eroded many basic protections against faulty identifications and has fostered a sense of confusion.

In the reform section, I will show how these conditions—psychological, procedural, and legal—create the dire need for eight specific reforms, two of which having never before been suggested in the misidentification literature. Additionally, unlike previous published recommendations for reform, which mostly aim at reducing misidentifications, my suggestions here take an additional approach by forcefully placing protections at the trial stage with the

---

[19] Koosed, Margery Malkin. 279.
[20] Ibid. 285.

acknowledgement that no amount of modified police procedure will eliminate the danger of misidentifications.

Finally, upon analyzing the failure of almost all past reform efforts, I will recommend that the eight reforms be implemented by state law and not left to local discretion, as they have been.[21] Thus, in specifics, scope, and suggested implementation, the reforms I propose here go significantly beyond what has already been proposed. All in all, these reforms follow logically from the forthcoming analysis of misidentification's causes and dangers.

Chapter 1.1: Current Police Procedure for Eyewitness Identification

When there is a witness who claims to have seen the crime or perpetrator, there are a number of steps the officer can take to determine whether the eyewitness recognizes the suspect as the perpetrator. The two most common methods are called show-ups and lineups.[22] While other methods exist, they are far less prevalent.[23] Both methods have a number of variations.

Show-ups involve the officer bringing the witness to the suspect and asking the witness whether he or she recognizes the suspect as the perpetrator. This can involve a one-suspect show-up, during which the witness is shown only one individual, or a series of show-ups, during which the witness is shown different suspects at different times. Most show-ups, however, involve only one suspect and occur shortly after the crime in question.[24]

In the majority of show-ups, after the crime has occurred and the police have apprehended a possible suspect, the witness will be brought to the suspect and asked whether the suspect is the perpetrator.

---

[21] Specifically, instead of urging local agencies to implement these policies, it should be accomplished through a state law.

[22] Wells, Gary L. "Eyewitness Identification: Systemic Reforms." 615.

[23] Ibid.

[24] Steblay, Nancy K. Mehrkens. "Reforming Eyewitness Identification: Cautionary Lineup Instructions; Weighing the Advantages and Disadvantages of Show-Ups Versus Lineups." Cardozo Public Law, Policy and Ethics Journal, April 2006, 348.

As one might expect, this procedure often involves a great deal of suggestiveness. The suspect may be in shackles, and the witness may believe that the police already have other evidence linking the suspect to the crime. In fact, "courts generally hold that one-to-one show-ups are presumptively suggestive" and may "constitute the most grossly suggestive identification procedure now or ever used by the police."[25] This and a number of other problems with show-ups will be outlined in depth in the following sections. Despite these issues, show-ups regularly take place in nearly every police department in the country.[26]

Furthermore, while the show-up procedure may contribute to misidentification, there are strong arguments for its use in some extreme cases. For example, if a witness may die at the scene of a crime, a show-up may be necessary. Additionally, a show-up at the scene between a witness and a suspect arrested blocks away could quickly exonerate the individual and allow the police to "scour the environs and pursue other leads."[27] Nonetheless, the pressures for show-ups do not eliminate the problems associated with the method.

One way of avoiding some of the suggestiveness of show-ups is to use lineups. Lineups involve the eyewitness viewing a number of individuals and noting whether any of them is the perpetrator of the crime. Lineups also regularly involve photographs. The most common form of lineup is the simultaneous lineup, during which the witness views three to six individuals (or photos), one of whom being the suspect and two to five of whom being "filler" individuals. These fillers are usually plainclothes officers or criminals whom the investigators know are uninvolved in the crime. As the psychological data will later indicate, the simultaneous lineup often encourages witnesses to make relative judgments (i.e., "which photo looks most

---

[25] Gambell, Suzannah. "The Need to Revisit the Neil v. Biggers Factors: Suppressing Unreliable Eyewitness Identifications." Wyoming Law Review, 2006, 193; Taylor, Lawrence. "Eyewitness Identification" at § 5-2, 1982 (citing Patrick M. Wall. "Eyewitness Identification in Criminal Cases." Charles C. Thomas, 1965, 28).
[26] Wells, Gary L. "Eyewitness Identification: Systemic Reforms." 615.
[27] Zanzini, John and Brownlow Speer. "Eye-Witness Identification After Commonwealth v. Martin: Two Views." Boston Bar Journal, January 2007, 7.

like the perpetrator?") rather than absolute judgments (i.e., "which photo, if any, shows the perpetrator?").[28] This encouragement of relative judgment is one of the primary criticisms of simultaneous lineups.

A final variant of the lineup is the sequential lineup, during which the witness views photos one at a time and makes an absolute judgment (i.e., "yes" or "no") for each one before proceeding to the next photograph. However, the sequential lineup is infrequently used.[29] Other procedures usually involve some variation of the above-listed procedures, such as a lineup photo book, which may show a hundred pictures, only one of which depicting the suspect. Overall, the most common procedures, in order of use, are the simultaneous lineup, the show-up, and the sequential lineup.[30]

[28] Ibid.
[29] Ibid.
[30] Ibid.

Chapter 2

PROBLEMS WITH WITNESS IDENTIFICATION

Witness misidentification accounts for such a large percentage of faulty capital convictions (50–75 percent) because of a number of identification problems.[31] This chapter will outline the underlying psychological studies and principles that lead to misidentification, show how police procedures exacerbate this phenomenon, identify further difficulties with cross-racial identifications, and then explain the procedural roadblocks that prevent juries from being made aware of these issues. Notably, the majority of this chapter will be devoted to the police procedure subsection.

Chapter 2.1: General Psychological Studies and Principles

Eyewitness memories are extremely fallible, and psychological study after study shows this. Specifically, the limitations of human memory—such as the use of relative judgment—lead to the high number of mistaken identifications. And, perhaps just as dangerously, several common-sense assumptions regarding reliability cues—including witness confidence and incident stress level—are flat-out wrong.

Compared to other types of forensic evidence, eyewitness testimony is the least reliable by far. One meta-analysis study found that, while polygraph experts "resolve 95% of cases correctly," handwriting experts resolve 94 percent of cases correctly, and fingerprinting experts resolve 100 percent of cases correctly, eyewitnesses, by contrast, resolve only 64 percent of cases correctly.[32] Simply speaking, this means that in the other 36 percent of eyewitness cases, the eyewitness is incorrect. The vast majority of psychological studies confirm this high rate.

---

[31] Koosed, Margery Malkin. 279; Wells, Gary L. "Eyewitness Identification Evidence: Science and Reform." 12.

[32] Wells, Gary L. "Eyewitness Identification: Systemic Reforms." 622–623.

In one particular study with a dramatized crime, when witnesses were presented with a six-person lineup on the same day as the dramatization, 54 percent of the witnesses identified the culprit, 21 percent made no identification, and 25 percent implicated one of the innocent fillers.[33] Therefore, among those witnesses who chose an individual, 32 percent chose the wrong one. Eyewitness identification experts and psychologists describe "relative judgment" as one of the major reasons for this high mistake rate.[34]

Relative judgment refers to the fact that witnesses will often select the lineup member who most resembles the culprit. Psychologists find that, instead of using absolute judgment, witnesses implicate suspects based on how they look relative to other lineup members.[35] This has a number of dangerous implications, primarily that—in any lineup—there will always be someone who looks more like the offender than the other fillers.[36] When the offender is present, he or she will most likely be selected, although the mistake rate is still around 30 percent. The biggest problem, however, arises when the offender is absent. It is then that witnesses will select innocent fillers, even when told that the culprit may not be present on the lineup. This has particularly dangerous implications, given that police have no burden to meet when choosing members of a photo lineup. They may place an individual's photo in the lineup based merely on a hunch or happenstance.

In layman's terms, this means that, when a culprit is not present in a lineup, a witness will likely select an innocent filler who most resembles the culprit, relative to the other innocent fillers, as the guilty culprit.

Indeed, psychological and field studies show that in culprit-absent lineups, witnesses positively implicate an innocent individual

---

[33] TerBeek, Calvin. 28.
[34] Wells, Gary L. "Eyewitness Identification: Systemic Reforms." 618.
[35] TerBeek, Calvin. 28.
[36] Wells, Gary L. "Eyewitness Identification: Systemic Reforms." 618–619.

nearly two thirds of the time.[37] The crime dramatization experiment mentioned above also tested witnesses with culprit-absent lineups. In these lineups, when asked to identify whether the culprit was in the lineup, 32 percent of witnesses correctly made no identification. However, 68 percent of witnesses selected one of the innocent fillers.[38] In a similar study of seventy-three store clerks, experimenters posed as customers and walked through stores exhibiting "memorably bizarre behavior." When asked hours later to identify the bizarre-acting "customer" from a photo spread, the clerks implicated filler photos in 34 percent of cases, even when told the customer may not be pictured.[39] Dozens of other studies show the same results: even when witnesses feel confident enough to positively identify the culprit they saw, these witnesses often get it wrong.[40] In lineups where the culprit is not present, witnesses get it wrong at a shockingly high rate.[41] And in almost all cases of lineups, the subconscious use of relative judgment means that witnesses are partly basing their decisions on other lineup participants instead of relying solely on their own memories.[42]

Moreover, while the use of relative judgment is probably the largest psychological problem associated with faulty lineup identifications, it isn't the only one. Elizabeth Loftus, a leading researcher in eyewitness identifications, discovered another psychological cause of mistaken identifications: "unconscious transference."[43] Unconscious transference occurs when a witness recognizes an individual but confuses the source of that recognition. In criminal cases specifically, unconscious transference will occur when a witness recognizes a person from a non-criminal incident but—upon seeing the person again in the lineup or show-up—mistakenly

---

[37] Ibid.
[38] TerBeek, Calvin. 28.
[39] Clements, Noah. 273.
[40] Ibid.
[41] Ibid.
[42] TerBeek, Calvin. 28.
[43] Gambell, Suzannah. 201.

remembers that individual as the perpetrator of the witnessed crime.[44] While the witness's familiarity with the suspect may be from passing him or her at a bus stop or frequently seeing the indigent suspect begging at street corners, this familiarity is unconsciously transferred to the face of the culprit at the scene of the crime.

Furthermore, unconscious transference can even occur in the absence of a past encounter between the witness and the suspect. Sometimes, just talking about the perpetrator can induce a type of transference. In one study, several subjects were placed within sight of a dramatized crime while others were placed near the crime location but out of sight of the crime and culprit. The experimenters then convened the "witnesses" and "non-witnesses" to discuss the crime for several hours. Following this, all participants were given an opportunity to identify the suspect from the lineup. A shocking 30 percent of the non-witnesses opted to identify the suspect, saying that they had witnessed the event.[45] This was in spite of the fact that none of the non-witnesses had been able to see the crime or culprit. In this study, unconscious transference produced manufactured "memories" of the incident in the minds of the non-witnesses.

Unconscious transference, relative judgment, and the significant fallibility of memory all help explain the high error rate among eyewitnesses. However, the faulty analysis of "post-identification cues" may be just as pernicious in increasing the danger of false identifications. Post-identification cues refer to circumstances that police officers, lawyers, judges, and juries use to determine the accuracy of an identification. Notably, nearly all studies on the subject show that common sense and the binding case law frequently lead decision makers in the exact opposite direction when it comes to evaluating accuracy based on two cues in particular, witness confidence and incident stress.

---

[44] Ibid. 201.
[45] Clements, Noah. 273.

It seems reasonable to believe that witness confidence can be a proxy for accuracy of identifications. After all, a witness who took a good, long look at the culprit—and committed the culprit's face to memory—would naturally be more confident in his identification. Indeed, current California case law on evaluating eyewitness identifications mentions witness confidence as a proxy for accuracy. However, the psychological data show that confidence bears little relation to accuracy.[46] "If there is one thing that the research is virtually unanimous on," a meta-analysis concludes, "it is this: there is no correlation whatsoever between eyewitness certainty and accuracy."[47] While not all studies conform to this conclusion, those that find a minor correlation also find that this correlation is vastly overshadowed by other confounding factors.

Instead of being based on accuracy, witness confidence is mostly based on "confirmatory feedback from police, post-event information, and supportive influence of other witnesses."[48] Gary Wells, a scholar in the field of eyewitness identification, found that positive feedback had "strong effects on the witnesses' retrospective reports" of confidence, among other things.[49] And while confidence is positively correlated with other "recalled" details regarding the event, these details are no more accurate than the identification itself.[50] In other words, a confident witness may subconsciously create details because his or her confidence level requires them to. These details, however, are "probably 'filled in' and inaccurate."[51] In short, despite what common perception and case law may say on the matter, as long as other spurious factors determine confidence, it cannot be used as a proxy for accuracy.

---

[46] Gambell, Suzannah. 202.
[47] Clements, Noah. 282.
[48] Kolbuchar, Amy, et al. "Improving Eyewitness Identifications: Hennepin County's Blind Sequential Lineup Pilot Project." Cardozo Public Law, Policy and Ethics Journal, April 2006, 390.
[49] TerBeek, Calvin. 26.
[50] Gambell, Suzannah. 202.
[51] Ibid.

By using confidence as a post-identification cue, decision makers regularly assume that there is a strong positive correlation between confidence and accuracy. In actuality, the correlation is negligible, if existent at all. With another post-identification cue, stress or trauma at the incident, the danger is even greater. This is because decision makers assume a strong positive correlation with accuracy when, in fact, a strong negative correlation exists.[52]

One of the common criticisms of laboratory studies and other psychological experiments—such as the ones described above—is that they do not involve the same amount of attention-directing stress that focuses a crime witness's observations.[53] These critics rely on common sense to "assume that eyewitness memory is much better for actual witnesses because somehow the stress or fear improves memory."[54] Indeed, even the binding case law on the matter—which, along with its problems, will be discussed in detail later—indicates that "the witnesses' degree of attention," measured partly by stress level, reflects a higher level of accuracy.[55] Once again, on the issue of witness stress and trauma, common sense and case law are at odds with psychological data. The data clearly indicate that stress reduces the witness's capacity to accurately recall faces and events.[56]

Several prominent studies show the negative effect of stress on accuracy. One study on the subject involved 509 Navy and Marine officers in a military survival training program. The officers were extensively interrogated for forty minutes in either a high-stress or a low-stress interrogation. Twenty-four hours later, the officers were asked to identify their interrogators out of a lineup. The accuracy rate for the high-stress scenario officers was 30 percent, while the accuracy

---

[52] Clements, Noah. 273–274; Gambell, Suzannah. 198; Wells, Gary L. "Eyewitness Identification Evidence: Science and Reform." 13.
[53] Wells, Gary L. "Eyewitness Identification Evidence: Science and Reform." 13
[54] Ibid.
[55] Gambell, Suzannah. 206.
[56] Clements, Noah. 273–274; Gambell, Suzannah. 198; Wells, Gary L. "Eyewitness Identification Evidence: Science and Reform." 13.

for the low-stress officers was 62 percent.[57] The same accuracy split existed in a sequential photo lineup (when the photos were presented one at a time). In both instances, the officers questioned in the low-stress interrogation had a significantly higher accuracy rate.[58] Conversely, and more significantly, the high-stress interrogations yielded double the rate of mistaken identification.[59] In another study, in which subjects watched violent and non-violent tapes, the subjects who watched the traumatic, violent tapes had "significantly worse" recall abilities.[60] Both studies demonstrate how stress and exposure to trauma have a negative effect on witness accuracy.

Stress and anxiety can decrease a witness's "perceptual scope and acuity," directing his or her attention in ways that limit facial recognition.[61] Perceived threat or danger can distract a witness from details that are not directly related to the threat, such as the features of the perpetrator's face. "Weapon focus" is an example of this phenomenon.[62] When a weapon is present, witnesses are inclined to stare at the weapon during the majority of the encounter. The weapon focus "distracts the witness" and "often results in an incorrect eyewitness identification."[63] In fact, studies have found that "up to fifty percent of identifications made when a weapon was present during the crime are incorrect."[64] Weapon focus supports the past studies that show how accuracy is inversely related to witness stress and trauma, despite what common perception and case law may say.

The psychological data is clear: witness memories are far more fallible than one might believe. Relative judgment and unconscious transference play tricks on the mind, resulting in mistaken identifications and failed memories. And common-sense cues as to

---

[57] Clements, Noah. 273–274.
[58] Ibid.
[59] Wells, Gary L. "Eyewitness Identification Evidence: Science and Reform." 13.
[60] Gambell, Suzannah. 198.
[61] Ibid.
[62] Ibid.
[63] Ibid.
[64] Ibid.

reliability are often just plain wrong, especially when it comes to witness confidence and the assumed greater accuracy from stressful, traumatic incidents.

Chapter 2.2: Police Procedures that Exacerbate Mistaken Identification

In addition to the fundamental psychological problems, witness misidentifications are also facilitated by police actions. The two main methods of eyewitness identification—the show-up and the simultaneous lineup—substantially increase the danger of misidentification. This is mainly because of police- and procedure-suggestiveness, biased instructions, the use of relative judgment, and other inherently error-prone aspects of these two methods. Additionally, even some types of sequential lineups have similar problems. Indeed, these faulty methods not only allow misidentifications but also strengthen witnesses' mistaken beliefs.

Police investigators have relatively stringent standards for forensic evidence, governing how it is collected, stored, and retrieved, including chain-of-custody rules for physical evidence.[65] Granted, investigators cannot interact with "eyewitness evidence" as they can with other forensic evidence. However, it is telling that there are almost no evidentiary standards for the collection of eyewitness identification evidence, even though its potential for contamination is as high as that of many other type of forensic evidence.[66] Witness identification procedures are based on custom and common practice, not scientifically developed theories on how to best ensure accuracy and reliability. This is especially dangerous given the number of possible ways an innocent person could find himself or herself in a lineup. An erroneous tip, a match in clothing, a coincidental link to the crime scene, or even an officer hunch are all examples of how an

---

[65] Wells, Gary L. "Eyewitness Identification: Systemic Reforms." 623.
[66] Ibid. 622–623.

innocent suspect's freedom can depend on police practice and identification accuracy.[67]

Of the two main identification formats, show-up and lineup, the show-up has the greatest potential for misidentification. Besides being the "most grossly suggestive identification procedure now or ever used by the police," show-ups fail to offer any real test of the witness's memory.[68] This inherent suggestiveness—and the lack of any memory test—helps explain why show-ups have the highest rate of misidentification out of all suspect-identification methods.[69]

Show-ups are inherently suggestive. They usually involve an officer bringing the witness to the suspect and asking something to the effect of, "Is this the culprit?"[70] As this meeting frequently occurs shortly after the police have arrived on the scene and begun their investigation, the suspect may be in handcuffs, in a police car, or in some other position suggesting criminality. Indeed, the "characteristics of the situation may convince the witness that the police have good reason to hold the apprehended individual."[71] Additionally, as psychology professor and show-up expert Nancy Steblay notes, the show-up instruction "implicitly requests a confirmation" when the police officers mention that they have picked up a suspect.[72] "The pressure to validate [the show-up] may be difficult to resist."[73] The suggestion of culpability and the pressure to affirm the officer's selection both push witnesses to positively identify the suspect shown, regardless of the strength of the witness's recollection.

This leads to the second major problem inherent with show-ups: the lack of a real memory test. Show-ups do not involve any mechanism to test how well the witness remembers the culprit. By contrast, lineups often use five "filler" individuals to "draw any errors

---

[67] Ibid. 620.
[68] Gambell, Suzannah. 193.
[69] Wells, Gary L. "Eyewitness Identification: Systemic Reforms." 628.
[70] Steblay, Nancy K. Mehrkens. 344.
[71] Ibid. 349.
[72] Ibid.
[73] Ibid.

away from the suspect and toward the fillers."[74] This is particularly important given the psychological data discussed above, which indicated that the rate of misidentification for a lineup is often somewhere around 35 percent.[75] Fortunately, this approximately 35-percent error rate is split among the five filler individuals in the lineup. With the show-up, however, this extra protection for innocent suspects isn't there. Any error will implicate an innocent suspect, as there are no fillers in show-ups.[76] The lack of memory testing "filler" individuals is a major reason for the high rate of show-up misidentifications.[77]

Nonetheless, police officers, prosecutors, and other officials point to the law-enforcement benefits that show-ups provide.[78] Show-ups provide officers with immediate information, often at the scene of the crime and usually before the resources for a photo or live lineup are available. They also protect the public from dangerous criminals. Without a positive identification, officers may not have enough evidence to take a potential murder suspect off the streets. Additionally, show-ups yield negative responses more than positive ones. This can free an innocent suspect while also freeing law enforcement to pursue other leads.[79] Supporters of show-ups also note that certain aspects of the show-ups may improve accuracy. Specifically, show-ups allow the witness to view the full body of the suspect (unlike photo lineups), displaying "gait, posture, affect, demeanor, and other attributes that may aid identification."[80] Show-ups also employ absolute, rather than relative, judgment. And, perhaps most importantly, show-ups usually occur very soon after the crime, leaving less time for the witness's memory to fade.

---

[74] Ibid.
[75] TerBeek, Calvin. 28; Wells, Gary L. "Eyewitness Identification: Systemic Reforms." 622–623.
[76] Steblay, Nancy K. Mehrkens. 350.
[77] Wells, Gary L. "Eyewitness Identification: Systemic Reforms." 628.
[78] Steblay, Nancy K. Mehrkens. 348–349.
[79] Zanzini, John and Brownlow Speer. 7.
[80] Steblay, Nancy K. Mehrkens. 349.

Still, while the law-enforcement-related arguments may have merit, the accuracy-related arguments fall relatively flat, as show-ups still have the highest rate of error among all common identification methods. Therefore, no matter how much timeliness and a full view of the suspect may help a witness, show-ups still yield misidentifications at a disproportionate rate. Furthermore, even the law enforcement arguments cannot mitigate the remarkably high rate of misidentifications that come from the show-ups' inherent suggestiveness and absence of a memory test. This is especially the case when one considers how modern technology—including digital photo databanks—could resolve most of the issues related to the need for immediate identification.

Indeed, to fully appreciate the magnitude of show-up error rates, it is useful to examine these error rates next to the error rates for the most common identification procedure, the simultaneous lineup. While simultaneous lineups have their own set of problems that can lead to misidentification, they still yield accurate results at a far higher rate than show-ups. To compare the misidentification rates of show-ups versus lineups, a meta-analysis surveyed twelve studies with a total of 3,013 participant witnesses.[81]

The initial data indicated some of the benefits of show-ups, including a lower "choosing rate." Witnesses felt confident enough to identify (or choose) a culprit in 44 percent of simultaneous lineups and 27 percent of show-ups.[82] This shows some of the increased cautiousness among witnesses in show-ups, likely due to the use of absolute versus relative judgment. However, once witnesses chose to identify a suspect, the studies indicated that an innocent suspect would be identified as the culprit in 15 percent of show-ups and 7 percent of simultaneous lineups.[83] That is, innocent suspects were twice as likely to be falsely identified in show-ups.

---

[81] Ibid. 350.
[82] Ibid.
[83] Steblay, Nancy K. Mehrkens. 353. The findings of this study are adapted with the assumption that all lineups would be six-person lineups with five fillers. Page 350

Now, one might wonder why the innocent misidentification rate was only 7 percent in lineups while the psychological data in the previous section put the lineup error rate at around 30 to 45 percent. The solution to this apparent contradiction lies in the distinction between the "general error rate" and the "dangerous error rate." The general error rate refers to the number of times a witness selects someone who isn't the culprit, which can include the "fillers" in lineups who are known by officers to be uninvolved in the crime. The dangerous error rate, by contrast, refers to the number of times a witness selects an innocent suspect whom the police are considering.[84] That is, a lineup selection of one of the fillers would add to the general error rate of lineups but not to the dangerous error rate. With show-ups, however, the general error rate and the dangerous error rate are the same, as any erroneous identification will be of the innocent suspect. The meta-analysis found a 43-percent general error rate for simultaneous lineups, which, split among six individuals, would yield a 7-percent dangerous error rate for the one innocent suspect under investigation.[85] The show-up's 15-percent general error rate would not be split among fillers and would, therefore, yield a 15-percent dangerous error rate.[86]

Show-ups compare even less favorably when the designated innocent suspect looks "similar" to the real culprit.[87] A similar-looking innocent suspect raises the show-up error rate by an additional 23 percent while raising the lineup error rate by an additional 17 percent.[88] Because this additional 17-percent lineup error is almost all due to the similar-looking innocent suspect, it is not split among the five fillers. However, the increase is still much larger for show-ups, and the resulting dangerous error rates are 38 percent for show-ups and

---

indicates that with only "three or four" fillers, the rate of dangerous error for simultaneous lineups may be as high as 15 percent.

[84] Ibid. 350.

[85] Ibid. 353.

[86] Ibid. 350.

[87] Steblay, Nancy K. Mehrkens. 351; Zanzini, John and Brownlow Speer. 6–7.

[88] Steblay, Nancy K. Mehrkens. 351.

24 percent for lineups. Furthermore, it must be noted that the twelve studies in this meta-analysis all involved show-ups that were as non-suggestive as possible. In addition to no "clothing similarity, suspect nervousness, and/or display of the suspect in the squad car or with handcuffs," the witness instructions were non-biased and did not indicate an officer's belief as to whether the suspect was the culprit.[89] Unlike in the studies, all of these listed absent conditions are likely in actual show-ups.[90]

Not only are show-ups suggestive, inadequate tests of memory, and powerful mechanisms for misidentification, they also yield misidentifications at a substantially higher rate than simultaneous lineups. However, just because simultaneous lineups are better than show-ups doesn't make them effective against the dangers of misidentification. The lineups' 7-percent dangerous error rate in the previous meta-analysis (24 percent with a similar-looking culprit) occurred in a setting of non-biased instructions and non-suggestive conditions. Indeed, as the past psychological and field studies indicate, the average rate of general error in simultaneous lineups hovers around 30 to 45 percent. This average incorporates far higher rates of error that are associated with a number of dangerous yet "acceptable" practices. For example, with fewer than five fillers—some police departments use as few as "three or four"[91]—this rate of error is spread across even fewer individuals, increasing the rate of dangerous error. With simultaneous lineups being the most common identification procedure, these high rates represent significant chances for misidentification.

Besides the general fallibility of memory, the misidentification potential with simultaneous lineups is associated with three aspects of the lineup: suggestion, incomplete instructions, and the use of relative judgment. The first two possible lineup aspects can raise the rate of error to levels significantly higher than those found in non-suggestive,

---

[89] Gambell, Suzannah. 216; Steblay, Nancy K. Mehrkens. 352.
[90] Gambell, Suzannah, 216; Steblay, Nancy K. Mehrkens. 352.
[91] Steblay, Nancy K. Mehrkens. 353.

non-biased psychological experiments, and the third aspect—relative judgment—will hold out the potential for misidentification regardless of the caution, safeguards, or vigilance of lineup administrators. Notably, this discussion will regard both live and photo lineups, as "all of the problems found in [live] lineups are nearly identical with the issues in photographic lineups or spreads."[92]

One of the causes of misidentifications in simultaneous lineups is the presence of suggestion.[93] Lineup suggestion is both conscious and—more commonly—unconscious. One common source of suggestion in the lineup is the police officer's actions. The police officer may give subtle, unintentional hints to the witness.[94] For example, the officer may change his posture, raise his eyebrows, or lean inward when the witness's gaze moves from a filler to the suspect. He or she may also ask, "Are you sure?" if the witness mentions a filler, or the officer might exclaim, "Yup, that's who we thought," if the witness mentions the suspect. Even "[s]eemingly innocuous gestures or phrasing by the investigator or subtle changes in procedure can dramatically affect the witness's thinking."[95]

Throughout the lineup, the officer exerts "enormous power over eyewitness behavior" not only in the witness's choice of whom to implicate but also in the decision of whether to make a choice at all.[96] Psychological data indicate that a witness's criterion for making a choice lies on a "continuum of cautiousness versus carelessness" and that the lineup's context, structure, and implementation all affect how cautious or careless the witness is in making a choice.[97] Lineups can be inherently suggestive, as witnesses often feel that the lineup has been set up because the culprit has been apprehended. Additionally, police behavior can make witnesses feel pressure to help the police,

---

[92] TerBeek, Calvin. 29.
[93] Clements, Noah. 287.
[94] Ibid. 279.
[95] Steblay, Nancy K. Mehrkens. 342.
[96] Ibid.
[97] Steblay, Nancy K. Mehrkens. 342.

cooperate in the investigation, and—accordingly—simply "trust their own memory."[98] Unfortunately, this often means making a choice when the haziness of the witness's memory prevents him or her from making the correct choice. In fact, one psychological study of simultaneous lineups found that even "subtle suggestion" that the culprit was present, when he was not, increased the choosing rate (and, therefore, the misidentification rate) to 90 percent (as every choice is a wrong one when the culprit is absent).[99] In short, suggestion inherent in the lineup and on the part of officers contributes considerably to the high misidentification rate.

Yet another contributing factor is the likelihood of incomplete lineup instructions. Specifically, in instructing witnesses for the lineup, many police departments do not tell the witness that the culprit may not be present in the lineup.[100] Some departments without this instruction may do without it because they find it unnecessary. Others may fear that the instruction will make the witness too cautious, thereby stopping the witness from making a correct identification.[101] In other cases investigators may be so confident of their suspect's guilt that they find the instruction pointless. Regardless of the reason, without the instruction, many witnesses will assume that the perpetrator must be in the lineup.[102] The use of relative judgment becomes more than a subconscious psychological process; in the witness's mind, it becomes the primary—if not only—means of selecting a lineup member. For the obvious and previously stated reasons, this is a dangerous phenomenon, as every lineup has someone who looks most like the culprit.

Indeed, biased instructions—that do not clarify the possible absence of the culprit—yield a substantially higher rate of misidentification. One study found that the simple instruction of "[the

---

[98] Ibid.
[99] Clements, Noah. 279.
[100] Steblay, Nancy K. Mehrkens. 343; TerBeek, Calvin. 28–29.
[101] TerBeek, Calvin. 29.
[102] Steblay, Nancy K. Mehrkens. 344.

culprit] may or may not be present" reduces the misidentification rate by 41 percent.[103] Another study found the accuracy to increase by 12 percent with proper instructions on the culprit's presence, with accuracy referring to the rate of correct identifications plus correct rejections.[104] Perhaps as significantly, these studies found no or negligible reductions in the rate of correct identifications. Upon hearing the instructions, witnesses did not become overly cautious to the point of no longer making correct identifications. In the first study, along with decreasing misidentifications by 41 percent, the rate of correct identification only fell by 1.9 percent.[105] The second study saw no effect on the rate of correct identifications.[106] Therefore, the absence or biases of these instructions is increasing the rate of misidentification without having any positive effect on correct identifications.

Suggestiveness and incomplete instructions contribute to the high rate of witness misidentification associated with simultaneous lineups. For the most part, these misidentification causes are directly associated with police action and, therefore, may be remediable. Unfortunately, however, the most significant defect of simultaneous lineups is inherent in the process: the facilitation of relative judgment. Even when witnesses are told that the culprit may be absent, and even when there is little pressure to make a choice when memory is weak, witnesses frequently use relative judgment, at least subconsciously.[107] The high misidentification rates associated with the psychological studies above—which usually employed proper instructions and non-suggestive implementation—are mostly attributed to the use of relative judgment.[108] The simultaneous lineup, by its very nature of presenting

[103] TerBeek, Calvin. 28–29.
[104] Steblay, Nancy K. Mehrkens. 347.
[105] TerBeek, Calvin. 29.
[106] Steblay, Nancy K. Mehrkens. 347.
[107] Wells, Gary L. "Eyewitness Identification: Systemic Reforms." 618.
[108] Clements, Noah. 273; Gambell, Suzannah. 201; Koosed, Margery Malkin. 279; TerBeek, Calvin. 28; Wells, Gary L. "Eyewitness Identification: Systemic Reforms." 622.

all members simultaneously, cannot avoid this natural subconscious psychological response.

Only with the use of absolute judgment can investigators minimize guessing by witnesses who are overconfident or motivated to appear useful.[109] "An effective lineup strategy must provide a careful test of memory alone," and simultaneous lineups fail in this task.[110] Fortunately, as discussed later in the chapter on reform, sequential lineups hold out the hope of doing just this: testing memory, not comparisons. Sequential lineups involve the presentation of photographs one at a time. For each photo, the witness is asked whether that photo shows the culprit. Without being allowed to view the previous "rejected" photos or the upcoming photos, witnesses are forced to make absolute judgments about each photo. A minority of police departments currently use sequential lineups as their primary identification method.[111]

While sequential lineups hold out the hope of avoiding relative judgment, improper execution of the sequential lineup can present some of the same problems for misidentification. Obviously, a suggestive setup or execution would pose the same danger to sequential lineups that it poses to simultaneous lineups. The same goes for incomplete instructions. However, sequential lineups, as they are currently being implemented, are also vulnerable to the danger of the same relative judgment of simultaneous lineups. This is because of a current sequential lineup practice called "laps."[112]

When witnesses go through the sequential lineup photos without identifying the suspect, the investigator will often allow the witness another "lap" through the photos.[113] With this second lap, the witness can go through all the photos again (usually six in number)

---

[109] Steblay, Nancy K. Mehrkens. 343.
[110] Ibid.
[111] Mecklenburg, Sheri, et al. "The Illinois Field Study: A Significant Contribution to Understanding Real World Eyewitness Identification Issues." *Law and Human Behavior*, February 2008, 1.
[112] Wells, Gary L. "Eyewitness Identification: Systemic Reforms." 627.
[113] Kolbuchar, Amy, et al. 397.

and then make an identification. Almost all jurisdictions that use sequential lineups allow laps, some allowing three, four, five, or even six laps.[114] When this occurs, the lineup becomes a "de facto simultaneous array, eliminating the sequential lineup's advantage."[115] Investigators use laps out of a worry that they may lose accurate identifications if they force "overly cautious eyewitnesses" to make their decisions without examining the photos a second time.[116] However, when laps are allowed, witnesses will likely "lapse into relative-judgment."[117]

Indeed, studies of sequential lineups show that, when laps are used, the rate of misidentification is significantly higher than the rate for non-lap sequential lineups.[118] The more laps, the higher the rate of misidentification. The following table of lap number and mistaken filler identification shows the general error rate ranging from 3 percent with one lap to a whopping 75 percent with four or more laps.

TABLE 1
Mistaken Identification Rate Based on Laps[119]

Laps	Filler ID	Lineups (n)
1	3%	68
2	10%	42
3	14%	14
4, 5, or 6	75%	4

Significantly, only four sequential lineups, or 3 percent, made it to the fourth or later lap. However, nearly half of the lineups

---

[114] Kolbuchar, Amy, et al. 398; Wells, Gary L. "Eyewitness Identification: Systemic Reforms." 627.
[115] Kolbuchar, Amy, et al. 397.
[116] Ibid.
[117] Ibid. 398.
[118] Wells, Gary L. "Eyewitness Identification: Systemic Reforms." 628.
[119] Kolbuchar, Amy, et al. 397–398.

involved at least one subsequent lap.[120] Additionally, another analysis of the same data found that, in cases where the witness did not personally know the culprit, the average rate of mistake was 29 percent for identifications that included more than two laps.[121] With laps through the photographs—and, therefore, the use of relative judgment once again—sequential lineups can face some of the same unacceptably high misidentification rates normally associated with simultaneous lineups and even show-ups.

At the very least, however, the use of laps—when recorded— provide some hints regarding the extent to which relative judgment is used.[122] The question for reformers, then, is how this information regarding reliability and relative judgment can be presented to the decision makers (investigators, defense attorneys, judges, and especially juries). This is yet another question to be answered in the reform chapter.

For now, most of the problems specifically associated with the three most common identification methods have been explored. However, one additional identification practice increases the danger of conviction based on misidentification: untimely confirmatory feedback. Untimely confirmatory feedback occurs when witnesses receive feedback confirming their identification and when this feedback comes before they state the circumstances surrounding their identification. Untimely confirmatory feedback can occur with any identification procedure, and it results in the jury's improper understanding of what the witness saw at the crime scene and how the witness acted during the show-up or lineup.[123]

The psychological section above discussed how witness confidence is not a proxy for accuracy because of the overshadowing

---

[120] Ibid. 398.
[121] Ibid.
[122] Kolbuchar, Amy, et al. 412; Wells, Gary L. "Eyewitness Identification: Systemic Reforms." 627.
[123] Kolbuchar, Amy, et al. 389–391; Steblay, Nancy K. Mehrkens. 342; TerBeek, Calvin. 25–26.

effects of confirmatory feedback. The same principle applies to a number of other factors judges and juries use to determine accuracy. Confirming and disconfirming feedback has "strong effects on the witnesses' retrospective reports of (a) their certainty [confidence], (b) the quality of the view they had, (c) the clarity of their memory, [and] (d) the speed with which they identified the person."[124] Positive feedback also buttresses witnesses' retrospective reports of their "degree of attention, their ease of identification, and of the basis for their identification." [125] These are all factors that juries rely on to determine identification accuracy—either due to legal instruction or common sense.

Notably, positive feedback can take many forms. Police comments after identification of a suspect can immediately shape the witness's views. Confirmatory feedback can also include later discussions with police officers and the eventual discovery that the witness's choice is being charged with the crime. All this knowledge is "untimely" because it is given before the witness is bound to a statement outlining his or her confidence, quality of view, clarity of memory, degree of attention, and other circumstances of identification. The confirmatory feedback almost guarantees that, once the witness relays his or her view of the crime and identification, the witness's retrospective report will be inflated. In short, without a mechanism for measuring the circumstances surrounding the identification and the witnessed event—before any positive response—confirmatory feedback will almost certainly distort the picture that the jury sees.

For the jury to have the most accurate facts, police procedure must treat eyewitness identification as the delicate evidence that it is. The inherent suggestiveness of show-ups and the absence of a memory test pose a significant danger for misidentification. The suggestiveness, incomplete instructions, and use of relative judgment also make simultaneous lineups less than ideal. A willingness to allow

---

[124] TerBeek, Calvin. 25–26.
[125] Kolbuchar, Amy, et al. 390–391.

subsequent laps also exposes sequential lineups to the drawbacks of relative judgment. And the powerful influences of confirmatory feedback can harm jury decision making, regardless of the identification method. In these ways, police procedures exacerbate the problems of witness misidentification.

Chapter 2.3: Problems with Cross-Racial Identifications

Police procedures are not alone in compounding the limitations of eyewitness identifications. Another factor builds on the underlying psychological factors to increase the likelihood of injustice: "own-race bias." Own-race bias refers to what experimental data have identified as "the unique difficulties that exist in recognizing faces of members of another race."[126] These unique difficulties can increase the rate of misidentification by as much as 56 percent and have a particularly large effect on black suspects.[127]

It may come as no surprise that racial factors disadvantage black defendants in the capital punishment system. Black individuals comprise 13 percent of the U.S. population, yet they make up 42 percent of the death row population.[128] While scholars present varying accounts of this phenomenon, studies indicate that the problems of cross-racial identifications play a significant role in death row's racial imbalance, especially among the falsely accused.[129] An Innocence Project report found cross-racial identifications to be "one of the leading causes of erroneous convictions" in the United States.[130]

The own-race bias posits that cross-racial identifications are subject to greater error and that this error is most pronounced when a white witness identifies a black suspect.[131] The own-race bias makes a witness more likely to falsely "remember" someone's face from

---

[126] Natarajan, Radha. "Racialized Memory and Reliability: Due Process Applied to Cross-Racial Eyewitness Identifications." New York University Law Review, November 2003, 1822–1823.

[127] Ibid. 1821.

[128] Solomon, Akiba. "A Matter of Life and Death." *Essence*, vol. 37, no. 1, May 2006, 138.

[129] Gambell, Suzannah. 200; TerBeek, Calvin. 26; Swams, Christina. "The Uneven Scales of Capital Justice." *The American Prospect*, vol. 15, no. 7, July 2004, A14.

[130] Natarajan, Radha. 1823.

[131] Gambell, Suzannah. 200.

another racial group, even if the witness has never seen that face before. This is ostensibly because "other-race faces" seem more similar to each other.[132] Some ascribe own-race bias to a partial inability of the witness to focus and remember facial features when confronted with an assailant from another race.[133] While the psychological cause of own-race bias is still unclear, there is "so much empirical evidence to support this [phenomenon] that it must be deemed, for all practical purposes, a fact."[134]

The "robust phenomenon" of own-race bias substantially increases the danger of misidentification, especially for black defendants.[135] Several studies on the subject found the rate of misidentification to increase by 56 percent when a white witness is presented with a black suspect—that is, the witness was 56 percent more likely to falsely remember the other-race suspect's face.[136] Additionally, these studies were non-suggestive, displaying yet another vexing issue associated with cross-racial identifications: the increased error rate cannot be addressed by general reforms, which do not "adequately protect defendants where there is a cross-racial identification."[137]

Not only do general reform efforts fail to diminish own-race bias, but "common-sense" proxies that jurors might use are also ineffective measures of witness accuracy. These false proxies are racial views, racial exposure, and response time.[138] Jurors—and other decision makers, including investigators—may assume that own-race bias only exists in racist witnesses. Furthermore, these decision makers may also assume that racial attitudes—or at least other-race exposure—may be correlated with the extent to which own-race bias exists in an individual. Both assumptions, however, are false.

The extent to which own-race bias affects identification accuracy is "unaffected by racial attitudes of the witness."[139] Racist or not, a witness's cross-racial identification has a substantially higher

---

[132] Natarajan, Radha. 1834.
[133] Gambell, Suzannah. 200.
[134] TerBeek, Calvin. 26.
[135] Natarajan, Radha. 1853.
[136] Ibid. 1834.
[137] Ibid. 1842.
[138] Gambell, Suzannah. 200; Natarajan, Radha. 1836.
[139] Gambell, Suzannah. 200; Natarajan, Radha. 1836.

likelihood of being erroneous. Furthermore, even "regular exposure to individuals of another race" does not diminish own-race bias.[140] And while some race-blind studies find witness response time (i.e., the speed of identification) to be a helpful proxy in determining accuracy, studies of cross-racial identification show that this proxy has no relation to accuracy in cross-racial identifications.[141] Needless to say, studies on own-race bias also find no relationship between confidence and accuracy.[142]

While racial attitudes, other-race exposure, and response time do not diminish own-race bias, there are two variables that demonstratively do. The bias is affected by the amount of time a witness views the culprit and the amount of time between the incident and the identification. While these two factors generally increase accuracy, they are particularly effective in reducing the effects of own-race bias.[143] The longer the witness views the culprit, the greater the witness's ability to accurately identify the culprit (at a rate commensurate with the accuracy rate of same-race identifications).[144] Similarly, the shorter the time period between the incident and the identification, the smaller the effects of own-race bias.[145] By the same token, shorter exposure and longer intervening time yield "more liberal" criteria for determining a match.[146]

These variables affecting cross-racial identification accuracy will be helpful in developing reforms intended to diminish or eliminate own-race bias, especially considering the general lack of current comprehensive reform plans that include protections against cross-racial misidentification.

---

[140] Gambell, Suzannah. 200.

[141] Natarajan, Radha. 1838–1839.

[142] Ibid. 1838.

[143] Ibid. 1836.

[144] Natarajan, Radha. 1836; Platz, Stephanie J. and Harmon M. Hosch. "Cross Racial/Ethnic Eyewitness Identification: A Field Study." Journal of Applied Social Psychology, vol. 18, no. 11, 1988.

[145] Natarajan, Radha. 1836.

[146] Ibid. 1837.

Chapter 2.4: Limitations in Presenting the Aforementioned Problems at Trial

The prior three subsections discussed the various phenomena and practices that lead to eyewitness misidentification. Yet another indirect problem arises when jurors are unaware of these potential dangers. Jurors are trusted to weigh the facts and use their judgment to find for guilt or innocence. However, when jurors' underlying beliefs and assumptions contradict the scientific or psychological data, the fair weighing of facts cannot occur, and the scale is tipped against innocent defendants.

Obviously, the primary problem of witness misidentification is the misidentification itself, not the mere fact that juries are ignorant of this phenomenon. Nonetheless, regardless of whatever procedural reforms are put in place, nothing can change the underlying psychological fallibility of witnesses' memories. Therefore, besides the procedural reforms addressing the identifications themselves, juries also need to at least know about these limitations to eyewitness testimony. Unfortunately, the traditional avenues for informing juries are largely closed to this type of information. Without sufficient knowledge of the psychological facts, jurors make two main mistakes: they have too much faith in eyewitnesses and, subsequently, rely on the wrong cues for accuracy.

Currently, jurors implicitly trust eyewitnesses.[147] Without knowledge of the psychological facts, jurors believe eyewitnesses "despite impeachment, despite aggressive cross-examination, and despite cautionary instructions."[148] Jurors even disregard any "information that challenges that faith," accepting eyewitness identifications as "absolute proof."[149] As a result, "there are more convictions than there are accurate identifications," which is a particular problem in cases where the life of the defendant is on the line.[150] Moreover, as attorney and reform advocate Noah Clements points out, even if jurors were more cautious in believing eyewitnesses,

---

[147] Clements, Noah. 284.
[148] Ibid. 284.
[149] Clements, Noah. 284; Gambell, Suzannah. 191.
[150] Clements, Noah. 284.

they wouldn't know what cues to use in differentiating between accurate and inaccurate testimony.[151]

Jurors "have little ability to make correct discriminations" because the cues they rely on do not correlate with accuracy.[152] In determining accuracy, jurors mostly use witness confidence, consistency, and memory of specific details, and none of those correlate with accuracy.[153] In a study of the use of confidence in predicting accuracy, for example, experimental jurors predicted that a "completely confident" witness had an 83-percent probability of being correct while a "somewhat uncertain" witness only had a 28-percent probability of being correct.[154] Jurors make similar assumptions based on witness consistency and memory of specific details, even though the former has no relation to accuracy and the latter is, in fact, "inversely correlated with accuracy."[155] In short, jurors have too much faith in eyewitnesses and—when questioning the eyewitness accounts—rely on the wrong cues.

The traditional avenues for informing juries are all severely limited in their ability to disabuse jurors of their incorrect notions. These traditional avenues include closing arguments, cross examinations, expert witnesses, and jury instructions. The closing argument, for example, is expressly limited to argument regarding facts that were presented in court. Any closing argument mention of scientific studies, which would almost certainly be inadmissible without an accompanying expert, would be improper.[156]

Cross examination is similarly ill-suited to deal with honest yet mistaken witnesses. While cross examinations can be very effective against dishonest or lying witnesses, they are "largely useless for detecting witnesses who are trying to be truthful but are genuinely mistaken."[157] Often, the harder attorneys press an apparently honest witness, the more sympathetic the witness appears in the eyes of the jurors.[158] And while attorneys can cross examine witnesses on

---

[151] Ibid. 285–286.
[152] TerBeek, Calvin.
[153] Clements, Noah. 285.
[154] Ibid.
[155] Ibid.
[156] Natarajan, Radha. 1843.
[157] Clements, Noah. 285–286.
[158] Ibid. 286.

psychological indicators of inaccuracy—such as a witness's identification response time, which is highly probative of accuracy in cross-racial identifications—these cross examination points will be meaningless to juries if they do not have the relevant psychological background material.

To inform juries of the scientific and psychological background relevant to eyewitness identifications, some defense lawyers call expert witnesses on the subject. Eyewitness identification expert witnesses are sometimes effective in making juries more wary of eyewitness testimony and helping them to use the right accuracy cues.[159] However, there are three main problems with expert witnesses in this field: they are often expensive, unavailable, and inadmissible.

Eyewitness experts are often too expensive for public defender offices, which represent the majority of death penalty defendants.[160] Furthermore, many defense attorneys are unaware of the psychological data that would make an eyewitness expert useful. Additionally, eyewitness identification experts are relatively rare.[161] There are only about fifty qualified eyewitness experts in the United States, many of whom do not testify in court on the matter, and those who do testify do so only a few times per year.[162] This makes it impossible to have an expert testify at a significant portion of the approximately 77,000 eyewitness identification cases that occur each year.[163] Furthermore, even if there were more experts, many courts prohibit them from testifying.[164] This prohibition will be discussed in further depth in the next chapter. Suffice it to say that expensive, unavailable, and inadmissible experts cannot help an incorrectly identified defendant.

Finally, jury instructions are equally limited in their ability to warn juries regarding eyewitness identifications.[165] Judges frequently read these jury instructions to jurors after the closing statements and before deliberation, and the instructions explain the law in wording that is supposedly easier to understand than the statute. However, as the instructions are usually just articulations of the law and

---

[159] Ibid.
[160] Wells, Gary L. "Eyewitness Identification Evidence: Science and Reform." 19.
[161] Ibid.
[162] Ibid.
[163] Ibid.
[164] Natarajan, Radha. 1833.
[165] Clements, Noah. 285; Gambell, Suzannah. 220; Natarajan, Radha. 1833.

procedure—and the law does not currently include any psychological principles or data—judges are not likely to include statements on issues like cross-racial identification or cues that correlate with accuracy.[166]

Therefore, in addition to the misidentification dangers themselves, juries are usually not even aware of these dangers. They unduly trust eyewitness testimony and rely on the wrong cues for accuracy. Closing statements, cross examinations, expert witnesses, and jury instructions are all ineffective in giving jurors the perspective they need to make accurate determinations.

---

[166] Clements, Noah. 285; Gambell, Suzannah. 220; Natarajan, Radha. 1833.

Chapter 3

WITNESS IDENTIFICATION CASE LAW

Naturally, decreasing the dangers of misidentification involves more than informing juries and asking police departments to change their practices. Besides police custom, courts have set out a number of vague rules governing what general types of identification practices are admissible in court. These rules are derived from case law—that is, they are rules based on various courts' interpretations of the law and the Constitution. A discussion of the relevant federal and state case law on the subject will help clarify the status of admissible witness identification practices. This discussion will revolve around the changing Supreme Court standard. Following this, an analysis of the case law's shortfalls can help explain the prevalence of eyewitness misidentification.

Chapter 3.1: Supreme Court Case Law Governing Witness Identifications

In *United States v. Wade* in 1967, the Supreme Court recognized the dangers of eyewitness identifications.[167] It found identifications themselves to be "proverbially untrustworthy."[168] And the Court went on to speculate that the dangerous impact of improper suggestion "probably accounts for more miscarriages of justice than any other single factor."[169] The Court even rebuked "Congress and other federal authorities" who had done nothing to reform procedures "even in the face of evidence" pointing to the dangers of current practice. Since these 1967 declarations, however, the court has shied away from tackling the problem, consistently watering down the standard for

---

[167] TerBeek, Calvin. 30 [citing *United States v. Wade*. 388 U.S. 218 (1967)].
[168] Ibid.
[169] TerBeek, Calvin. 30–31 (citing *Wade*); *United States v. Wade*. 388 U.S. 218, 229 (1967).

admissibility and even allowing procedures that are "unnecessarily suggestive," to use the Court's own words.[170]

This discussion of case law will trace the evolving Supreme Court standard for eyewitness identifications. The review will trace its evolution from the late 1960s to the late 1970s, at which point the standard arrived at its current form. Accompanying this will be a specific description of how the standard became narrower in scope over the years, encompassing fewer procedures and fewer periods in the crime-to-verdict timespan. After a short analysis of the Court's general rationale for these changes, an overview of state and appellate case law will survey the state of interpretation and implementation of the binding Supreme Court standard in various U.S. jurisdictions. The subsection following this will explain the specific problems that the current state of case law presents.

In broad terms, the current standard governing the admissibility of eyewitness identifications places two burdens on the defendant. In order to have eyewitness evidence suppressed, the defendant has to prove that the identification procedure was "unnecessarily suggestive" and that no subsequent identification from the witness is "independently reliable."[171] While the details will be discussed later, in short, this standard means that the defendant has to prove unnecessary suggestiveness in the procedure used and an unreliability on the part of the witness's testimony. But the standard did not start out this way. The Supreme Court's first broad criterion on eyewitness identification was established in two cases decided on the same day in 1967: *United States v. Wade* and *Stovall v. Denno.*[172]

In *United States v. Wade*, the Court found that witness identification procedure could violate a defendant's constitutional rights to due process and legal representation.[173] Violation of these

---

[170] *Neil v. Biggers.* 409 U.S. 188 (1972).

[171] Ibid.

[172] *Stovall v. Denno.* 388 U.S. 293 (1967); *United States v. Wade.* 388 U.S. 218 (1967).

[173] Gambell, Suzannah. 203–204; TerBeek, Calvin. 30.

Fifth and Sixth Amendment rights could result in the inadmissibility of the identification. Specifically, the court found that the defendant had a right to counsel during the lineup procedure. Noting how "the annals of criminal law are rife with instances of mistaken identification," the Court found the pre-trial identification procedure to be particularly important, requiring the presence of counsel.[174] Pre-trial identification "typically determines the identification at trial," and witnesses are "not likely to go back on [their] word later on."[175] Furthermore, the defendant cannot be expected to "effectively reconstruct at trial any unfairness that occurred at the lineup."[176] "Improper influences may go undetected" by the suspect and witness.[177] Defendants are, therefore, entitled to counsel as a necessary guard against these improper influences, which, left ignored, could violate a defendant's rights.

The Supreme Court presented a two-pronged remedy for situations when counsel was denied. First, if a defendant were denied counsel, the evidence of the initial out-of-court identification would be *per se* inadmissible. That is, if counsel was denied, no evidence would be admitted or allowed that references that initial, out-of-court identification. This means that the witness would also be prohibited from mentioning this earlier identification. This exclusion of pre-trial identifications was intended as a proportional response to the misconduct, given that a lineup without counsel may nonetheless be accurate.[178] Still, without some possibility of exclusion regarding the witness's in-court testimony, *Wade*'s standard would have been very limited. Indeed, this was the second prong of the court's remedy, which addressed whether a witness was allowed to make another identification, in the live courtroom, even if that witness had previously been exposed to an "illegal" lineup (as a lineup without counsel was now defined). The Court said that an in-court

---

[174] Gambell, Suzannah. 203 (citing *United States v. Wade*).
[175] Gambell, Suzannah. 203–204 (citing *United States v. Wade*).
[176] Koosed, Margery Malkin. 288 (citing *United States v. Wade*).
[177] Koosed, Margery Malkin. 288 (citing *United States v. Wade*).
[178] Koosed, Margery Malkin. 289.

identification was admissible only if the government could prove "by clear and convincing evidence that the in-court identifications were based upon observations of the suspect other than the lineup identification."[179] In short, the prosecution had to prove that the witness is not simply recalling the defendant because a suggestive procedure drew this witness to the defendant. Only by proving an independent source for the identification would the prosecution be allowed to elicit an in-court identification from the eyewitness.

In determining the independence of source, the Court emphasized the consideration of factors "such as the witness previously identifying a different suspect, the failure of the witness to identify the defendant previously, and the length of time between the identification and the crime."[180] Fundamentally, in *Wade* the Court recognized that the presence of defense attorneys could help offset some of the "vagaries of eyewitness identification" and the "innumerable dangers and variable factors which might seriously, even crucially, derogate from a fair trial."[181] *Wade* affirmed that pre-trial identifications often determine the fate of a defendant, and it created a two-pronged admissibility remedy for lineups during which counsel was unable to ensure fairness.

The right to counsel during lineups was a helpful step in combating suggestiveness during the identification procedure. However, the presence of counsel was no guarantee against even the most suggestive practices. This danger was addressed in *Stovall v. Denno*, which the Supreme Court decided on the same day as *Wade*.[182] The Court held that some identification processes can be "so unnecessarily suggestive and conducive to irreparable mistaken identification that [the defendant] was denied due process of law." [183] An "unnecessarily suggestive" procedure was one that employed

---

[179] Gambell, Suzannah. 203 [citing *Stovall v. Denno*. 388 U.S. 293 (1967)].
[180] Gambell, Suzannah. 204.
[181] Kolbuchar, Amy, et al. 384 (citing *Stovall v. Denno*).
[182] Koosed, Margery Malkin. 291–292.
[183] Gambell, Suzannah. 203 (citing *Stovall v Denno*).

suggestiveness without "an emergency or exigent circumstances that made the suggestive technique unavoidable."[184] Thus, *Stovall* explained two possible violations of a defendant's due process rights: the subjection to an "unnecessarily suggestive" identification procedure and—more significantly—the subjection to such a procedure that resulted in "substantial likelihood of irreparable mistaken identification."[185]

The lower courts have interpreted *Stovall* and *Wade* to set forth a two-pronged remedy for unnecessarily suggestive procedure.[186] If an unnecessarily suggestive procedure occurred during an identification, that out-of-court pre-trial identification would be *per se* inadmissible at trial. However, the eyewitness is allowed to testify and make an in-court identification as long as there is no "substantial likelihood of irreparable mistaken identification" as a result of the unnecessarily suggestive procedure.[187] Only if the procedure presents a "substantial likelihood" of mistaken identification is the court required to prevent the witness from making an in-court identification.

Wade and *Stovall* created this set of standards in 1967, and for several years these standards were modest yet forceful attempts to limit the dangers of eyewitness misidentifications. Pre-trial lineups required the presence of counsel and identification procedures could not be "unnecessarily suggestive." Any violation of these terms required exclusion of the out-of-court pre-trial identification in all cases and exclusion of the in-court identification when—essentially—there was a significant danger of misidentification as a result of the procedural violation. These safeguards did not last long, however, and the Supreme Court of the 1970s eroded the *Wade* and *Stovall* protections by limiting their scope, removing some of their remedies, and eventually watering down the standards themselves.

---

[184] Gambell, Suzannah. 205.

[185] Gambell, Suzannah. 206 (citing *Stovall v. Denno*).

[186] Koosed, Margery Malkin. 292.

[187] Koosed, Margery Malkin. 292–293 (citing *Brathwaite v. Manson*. 527 F.2d 363 (2d Cir. 1975) [quoting *Simmons v. United States*. 390 U.S. 377 (1968)]).

The dilution of the Supreme Court's eyewitness identification standards occurred in four main cases: *Kirby v. Illinois, United States v. Ash, Neil v. Biggers*, and *Manson v. Braithwaite*. The first two cases severely limited the meaning and effect of any *Wade* requirement for the presence of counsel. The two latter cases revised the test for an identification-related due process violation and created a new standard that, by definition, allows many types of "unnecessarily suggestive" procedures. As a result of these changes, as many eyewitness misidentification experts have pointed out, courts generally "use every conceivable method to avoid finding due process violations except in the most outrageous situations."[188] These 1970s cases are the end of the Supreme Court's comments on the eyewitness identification issue.

Under *Wade*, the right to counsel was one of the strongest protections against suggestive or otherwise improper identification procedures. Not only could defense attorneys re-create the improper lineup at trial, but they could also watch for any unnecessarily suggestive practices that might invoke *Stovall v. Denno*'s protections. Yet this powerful safeguard against improper procedure was severely limited just five years after the Court's *Wade* decision. In *Kirby v. Illinois*, the Court ruled that the Sixth Amendment right to counsel only applies after the defendant has been indicted.[189]

The right to counsel, according to the Court, only applied after the "critical stage" of indictment. This "initiation of judicial proceedings" is the "starting point of our whole system of adversary criminal justice."[190] It is only then that "the adverse positions of government and defendant have solidified."[191] In effect, *Kirby* removed the protection of counsel for the very period during which a lineup is particularly likely: when police are deciding whom to

---

[188] Gambell, Suzannah. (citing Grano, Joseph); Grano, Joseph. "Kirby, Biggers, and Ash: Do Any Constitutional Safeguards Remain After the Danger of Convicting the Innocent?" Michigan Law Review, no. 72, 1974, 717, 780.
[189] *Kirby v. Illinois*. 406 U.S. 682 (1972); TerBeek, Calvin. (citing *Kirby v. Illinois*)
[190] TerBeek, Calvin. (citing *Kirby v. Illinois*).
[191] Ibid.

investigate and prosecutors are deciding against whom to bring charges.[192] The Court argued that this change in Sixth Amendment applicability was an effort to balance the "rights of the accused" and the "interest of society in the prompt and purposeful investigation of an unsolved crime."[193] There may have been a fear among the members of the Court that requiring the presence of counsel would delay the lineup, as police officers would often have to wait for the court to assign counsel to indigent defendants.

Yet perhaps most striking about the *Kirby* ruling was what many saw as its irreconcilability with *Wade*'s stated rationale.[194] As cited earlier, *Wade* argued that the first identification between the witness and the suspect "typically determines the identification at trial" and that witnesses are "not likely to go back on [their] word later on."[195] Nothing indicates that pre-indictment lineups would be any different from post-indictment lineups in this respect. The same applies to the defendant's probable inability to detect "improper influences" in the lineup process and execution.[196] Nonetheless, the *Kirby* ruling limited the right to counsel, holding that the Sixth Amendment guarantee comes after the formal beginning of judicial proceedings indicated by the indictment.

The *Kirby* ruling limited *when* in time a lineup required the presence of defense attorneys. Within a year, in *United States v. Ash*, the Supreme Court limited *which* types of lineups required defense counsel.[197] This ruling removed the Sixth Amendment guarantee from what is now the most common lineup technique: the photo lineup.[198] The Court found that the "minimal risk" associated with photo lineups

---

[192] *Kirby v. Illinois*. 406 U.S. 682 (1972).
[193] TerBeek, Calvin. (citing *Kirby v. Illinois*).
[194] Gambell, Suzannah. 204; Koosed, Margery Malkin. 288.
[195] Gambell, Suzannah. 203–204 (citing *United States v. Wade*).
[196] Ibid.
[197] Kolbuchar, Amy, et al. 384.
[198] Personal Communications with Joseph Krakora, Assistant Public Defender for New Jersey.

did not require the presence of counsel.[199] Furthermore, the Court straightforwardly argued that whether counsel could help guarantee a fair trial was not even the question for consideration.[200] "The threshold question... is not whether counsel can guarantee a fair trial but whether the defendant required counsel's assistance in a confrontation with the procedural system or a skilled adversary."[201] That is, the purpose of counsel laid simply in his or her legal expertise and ability to navigate the defendant through the criminal justice system, not in his or her vigilance against improper or suggestive identification techniques.

The Court's conclusion in *Ash* was based partly on the "English common law procedures" on which the Sixth Amendment was based, which guaranteed counsel "at trial" when facing "the intricacies of the law and the advocacy of the public prosecutor."[202] Moreover, the Court asserted that the defense counsel is no more than an extension and agent of the defendant; therefore, as the defendant himself has no right whatsoever to be present at the photo lineup, it made little sense for the defense counsel to be entitled to attend.[203] Still, in adopting this interpretation of the purpose and extent of the Sixth Amendment guarantee, *Ash* ignored or discarded some of the very reasons for counsel that *Wade* trumpeted—namely, the ability to detect "improper influences," "reconstruct... unfairness," and otherwise offset the "vagaries" and "innumerable dangers" that can "derogate from a fair trial."[204]

While *Kirby v. Illinois* and *United States v. Ash* severely limited the scope and, therefore, the effectiveness of *United States v. Wade*'s standard, the 1972 case of *Neil v. Biggers* and the 1977 case of *Manson v. Brathwaite* did the same for *Stovall*. However, instead of

---

[199] Kolbuchar, Amy, et al. 384.
[200] Grano, Joseph. 761.
[201] Grano, Joseph. 761–762 [citing *United States v. Ash*. 413 U.S. 300 (1973)].
[202] Grano, Joseph. 761–762 (citing *United States v. Ash*); *United States v. Ash*. 413 U.S. 300, 309 (1973).
[203] Grano, Joseph. 762.
[204] Kolbuchar, Amy, et al. 384 (citing *United States v. Wade*).

merely limiting its applicability, *Biggers'* and *Brathwaite's* holdings effectively overturned the *Stovall* standard and created a new one, with *Biggers* creating the standard and *Brathwaite* establishing its universality.[205] Significantly, the new standard presented a higher burden for the defense, allowed many "unnecessarily suggestive" procedures, and shifted the focus from the procedure to the witness.[206]

Recall that *Stovall's* standard on "unnecessarily suggestive" identification procedures—as interpreted by lower courts based on *Stovall* and *Wade*—excluded the out-of-court identification in every instance and excluded an in-court identification if the procedure resulted in "substantial likelihood of irreparable mistaken identification."[207] The *Biggers* standard set forth a different two-pronged approach, requiring the defendant to prove both aspects in order to have eyewitness testimony excluded. First, the defendant must prove that the procedure was "unnecessarily suggestive." Second, the defendant must prove that the in-court identification is unreliable based on "the totality of the circumstances," which includes a number of circumstances the court put forth.[208]

The first change is immediately notable: there is no longer a *per se* exclusion of unnecessarily suggestive out-of-court identifications.[209] This not only means that these out-of-court identifications can be shared in court to support the prosecution's contention of witness accuracy and consistency, but it also means that police no longer have this powerful incentive against suggestiveness. Still, the most important identification is the one taking place in the courtroom, and that leads to the second major change in the standard.

---

[205] Koosed, Margery Malkin. 294–295.

[206] Ibid. 295; Gambell, Suzannah. 203; Kolbuchar, Amy, et al. 384.

[207] Gambell, Suzannah. 203 (citing *Stovall v. Denno*).

[208] There is some dispute as to where the burden lies for the second aspect of the *Biggers* two-pronged test. Most courts place the burden for both on the defendant (Koosed, Margery Malkin. 302; TerBeek, Calvin. 35). "Some" courts, however, place the burden for the second prong on the government (Koosed, Margery Malkin. 302).

[209] TerBeek, Calvin.

While the *Wade-Stovall* standard focused on the procedure and its suggestiveness in both prongs of the two-pronged approach, the new standard nearly ignores the procedure in its evaluation of witness reliability.

According to the *Biggers* standard, once a defendant has proven that an identification procedure was unnecessarily suggestive, the court must evaluate the reliability of the witness, and the court must do so by evaluating "the totality of the circumstances," which consists of five specific factors, none of which relates to potential suggestiveness. These factors are

> [1] the opportunity of the witness to view the criminal at the time of the crime,
> [2] the witness's degree of attention,
> [3] the accuracy of the witness's prior description of the criminal,
> [4] the level of certainty demonstrated by the witness at the confrontation, and
> [5] the length of time between the crime and the confrontation. [210]

As *Brathwaite* notes in its declaration of *Biggers'* universality, "reliability is the linchpin in determining the admissibility of identification testimony."[211] What's more, the *Biggers* test determines reliability based solely on input from the witness, some of which are self-reported, including factors one, two, and four. Therefore, regarding the second prong of the *Biggers-Brathwaite* standard, it no longer matters whether the identification procedure was "prejudicial to the criminal defendant." This alone will not affect the admissibility of any evidence, no matter the prejudicial extent. Furthermore, in determining accuracy, the factors related to the unnecessarily suggestive procedure are no longer relevant.

---

[210] Gambell, Suzannah. 203 (citing *Neil v. Biggers*).
[211] TerBeek, Calvin. 33 (citing *Mason v. Brathwaite*).

This new standard is the binding case law today. Its evolution through the 1970s has limited the right to counsel to post-indictment, non-photo lineups. Besides Sixth Amendment claims, the prospect for excluding identification evidence only exists when the defendant can show both unnecessary suggestiveness and a lack of reliability on the part of the witness. Significantly, because today's case law on eyewitness identification was settled in Supreme Court cases from 1972, 1973, and 1977, the Justices came to their decisions without the vast majority of the psychological and field data discussed earlier, which mostly surfaced in the 1980s and 1990s. However, before taking an in-depth look at the myriad problems this Supreme Court case law presents, it will be useful to analyze what different states and federal courts have done to interpret the Supreme Court's ruling and create their own state-level standards.

Chapter 3.2: Federal Circuit and State Case Law Governing Eyewitness Identifications

Federal circuit and state courts have come to a number of different conclusions about the meaning and implementation of the *Biggers-Brathwaite* standard. The federal disagreement lies in what other factors, if any, may be included with the traditional five factors listed in the *Biggers* standard. Many state courts take part in this debate as well, although some states have found the *Biggers* standard unconstitutional under their state constitutions or uninformed by the modern psychological studies on witness misidentification.

All the federal circuit courts use the *Biggers* standard to determine the admissibility of a witness's identification. However, as Suzannah Gambell points out in her article on the topic, the courts are split on whether the *Biggers* "totality of the circumstances" include a sixth factor that was "assumed" by the Supreme Court.[212] Ms. Gambell's description of the chaotic state of case law demonstrates an unclear state of case law on this issue, which, in turn, contributes to the

---

[212] Gambell, Suzannah. 206–208.

widely varying standards that courts use. Here, I use her examples from the circuit and state courts to show the absolute need for clarity.[213] For example, the First, Fourth, Seventh, and Eighth Circuit courts argue that a sixth factor for consideration is "corroborating evidence of general guilt," which may not be directly related to the reliability of the identification.[214] Generally speaking, the courts that view corroborating evidence of general guilt as a sixth factor argue that, if other evidence points to guilt, there is a higher likelihood that the identification was accurate. Furthermore, the courts reason that corroborating evidence diminishes the likelihood of a faulty conviction based solely on an eyewitness's mistake.[215] Three examples of sufficient corroborating evidence of guilt from the Seventh, Eighth, and First Circuits, respectively, include proof that a defendant drove a getaway car, testimony from other witnesses that identified the defendant, and ownership of the gun used in the robbery.[216] These would all be considered *Biggers* factors for indirectly evaluating the reliability of an eyewitness identification.

While not all circuit courts have taken a side on this issue, three have come out strongly against the use of corroborating evidence of general guilt as a sixth factor. The Second, Third, and Fifth Circuit courts reject the argument that facts unrelated to the identification can make it any more reliable. The Second Circuit has called this supposed sixth factor nonsensical, for "even when there was irrefutable evidence of a defendant's guilt, if an identification were made by a witness who, it transpired, was not even present at the event, we could hardly term

---

[213] For an updated list of the standards adopted by various federal and state courts, see Lawrence Rosenthal, "Eyewitness Identification and the Problematics of Blackstonian Reform of the Criminal Law," Journal of Criminal Law and Criminology, Vol. 110 (Forthcoming), footnotes 212 and 213.

[214] Gambell, Suzannah. 206–208.

[215] Ibid. 208.

[216] Gambell, Suzannah. [citing *United States ex rel. Kosik v. Napoli.* 814 F.2d 1151 (7th Cir. 1987); *United States v. Rogers.* 73 F.3d 774 (8th Cir. 1996); and 59 F.3d (1st Cir. 1995)].

the identification reliable."[217] Furthermore, the Third Circuit has argued that using this sixth factor of general guilt is irreconcilable with *Biggers'* test, which is focused exclusively on the reliability of the identification itself. The Circuit noted that "[i]ndependent evidence of culpability will not cure a tainted identification procedure, nor will exculpatory information bar admission of reliable identification testimony."[218] This split in interpretation has existed for many years, during which time almost all of the circuit courts have addressed the issue.[219]

Among state courts, the split is not nearly as pronounced, as only a limited number of states have recognized a sixth factor of general culpability.[220] For example, the Tennessee Court of Appeals in Nashville accepts corroborating evidence of guilt as a factor in *Biggers'* totality of the circumstances test, and it noted in 1994 that this type of evidence is often used throughout Tennessee courts in evaluating the admissibility of witness identifications.[221]

For a number of states, however, the debate has not been about how best to apply *Biggers* but about whether to apply *Biggers* at all. Indeed, several state supreme courts have flatly rejected the *Biggers* and *Brathwaite* standard as inadequately protecting the rights of defendants.[222] Moreover, these state courts—including Massachusetts, New York, Kansas, and Utah—have all shown an openness and willingness to "disagree with *Biggers* factors if they appear scientifically outdated."[223] Broadly speaking, these states have rejected the *Biggers* standard on one of two often overlapping grounds: they either find it unconstitutional under their state constitution's guarantee of due process or they find the factors listed to be incompatible with

---

[217] Gambell, Suzannah. 209 [citing *Raheem.* 257 F.3d 122, 141 (2d Cir. 2001)].
[218] Gambell, Suzannah. 210 [citing *United States v. Emanuele.* 51 F.3d 1123 (3d Cir. 1995)].
[219] Gambell, Suzannah. 211. See footnote 216, supra.
[220] See footnote 216, supra.
[221] Gambell, Suzannah. 213.
[222] Gambell, Suzannah. 211; TerBeek, Calvin. 50.
[223] Gambell, Suzannah. 211.

the psychological data on witness identification.[224] The standard used instead of *Biggers* is either a *per se* exclusionary rule for all "unnecessarily suggestive" procedures (the rule in Massachusetts and New York) or a modified *Biggers* standard with factors supported by the psychological data (the standard in Utah and Kansas).[225]

The Massachusetts Supreme Court has taken the toughest stance against unnecessarily suggestive identification procedures. The Massachusetts court could not re-interpret the U.S. Constitution's Fifth Amendment due process guarantee with respect to witness identifications (as the U.S. Supreme Court had already done this in *Biggers* and *Brathwaite*), but it could interpret its own state constitution. Basing its ruling on the Massachusetts constitution's due process guarantee, citing the post-1977 scientific evidence, and agreeing with Justice Marshall that "eyewitness testimony is often hopelessly unreliable," the court chose to make all "unnecessarily suggestive" identifications *per se* inadmissible.[226] The New York Court of Appeals ruled similarly.[227]

While not going so far as to reject *Biggers*, the Utah Supreme Court chose to modify the factors that went into the "totality of the circumstances," which, once again, is supposed to be used to determine the reliability of the identification. In *State v. Ramirez* in 1991, the court found the current five factors to be flawed, pointing out that "several of the criteria listed by the Court are based on assumptions that are flatly contradicted by well-established and essentially unchallenged empirical studies."[228] Noting that "the time has come for a more empirically sound approach," the Utah court set

---

[224] Gambell, Suzannah. 211; TerBeek, Calvin. 50; Zanzini, John and Brownlow Speer. 6.

[225] Gambell, Suzannah. 211–212.

[226] Ibid. 212.

[227] Ibid.

[228] Gambell, Suzannah. 211 [citing *State v. Hunt.* 69 P.3d 571 (Kan. 2003); *Commonwealth v. Johnson.* 650 N.E.2d 1257 (Mass. 1995); *People v. Adams.* 423 N.E.2d 379 (N.Y. 1981); and *State v. Ramirez.* 817 P.2d 774 (Utah 1991)].

forth a modified version of *Biggers*.[229] This modified standard removes the factor of witness confidence and adds the factor of the "suggestibility of the identification."[230] Kansas adopted this same standard in its 2003 case of *State v. Hunt*, although it noted that the holding "should not be considered as a rejection of the *Biggers* model, but, rather, as a refinement in the analysis."[231]

Recently, the Connecticut Supreme Court concluded "that it is appropriate to modify the *Biggers* framework to conform to recent developments in social science and the law,"[232] and the Vermont Supreme Court removed "witness certainty as a factor in assessing the reliability of a witness identification made in suggestive circumstances."[233]

Clearly, there is no case law consensus on how challenges to witness identifications should be treated. The states supreme courts disagree on how to protect the accused, the circuit courts disagree on how to interpret *Biggers*, and the United States Supreme Court of 1972 and 1977 seems to disagree with the Court of 1967 on what protections the Constitution affords. This has created confusion and inconsistency. More dangerously, however, this debate has its foundation in *Biggers, Brathwaite, Ash,* and *Kirby*. This foundation is inherently faulty, and the subsequent discussion will bring to light how this current binding case law substantially increases the danger of witness misidentification.

Chapter 3.3: Problems with Current Case Law

Simply speaking, the current case law for witness identification procedure does not match up with the scientific and psychological data on the subject. The "empirical research of the past thirty years" contradicts the Justices' intuitions as well as the resulting standard.[234]

---

[229] *State v. Ramirez*, 817 P.2d at 780.
[230] Gambell, Suzannah. 211 [citing *State v. Long*. 721 P.2d 483 (Utah 1986)].
[231] Gambell, Suzannah. [citing *State v. Hunt*, 69 P.3d 571, 577 (Kan. 2003)].
[232] *State v. Harris*, 191 A.3d 119, 134 (Conn. 2018).
[233] *State v. Discola*, 184 A.3d 1177, 1189 (Vt. 2018).
[234] TerBeek, Calvin. 35.

While case law is only one factor that effects the rate of witness misidentification, the currently binding Supreme Court decisions lead courts in the wrong direction, forcing a determination of reliability based on the wrong criteria. This analysis of the case law's shortfalls will involve a closer look at the *Biggers* standard, including its factors and its vague writing, which has yielded confusion among lower courts. An examination of the case law's results will follow, addressing the current incentives for police agencies and the documented rise in misidentifications that has ironically followed the *Kirby-Ash-Biggers-Brathwaite* wave of Supreme Court decisions.

The primary problem with the *Biggers* standard is that its factors for measuring accuracy do not, in fact, measure accuracy. Numerous law review articles and eyewitness identification experts have discussed this disconnect between the science and the standard, leading to "factors [that] are not scientifically linked to accuracy."[235] Moreover, the standard is "under-inclusive," failing to mention a number of other factors that are shown to correlate with accuracy.[236] Given how federal and state courts tend to view the *Biggers* list as exhaustive, this results in other relevant factors not being considered. Naturally, this disconnect between the literature and the law has something to do with the fact that nearly all of the major psychological studies on witness memory and misidentification have been published after 1980.[237] Since the 1977 case of *Manson v. Brathwaite*, the Supreme Court has not taken up this issue again, thus maintaining the same five factors that *Biggers* established.

Notably, this discussion of *Biggers'* failings will not address the issue of procedural fairness. Some critics of *Biggers*, including Justice Marshall himself, have described its standard as "not particularly concerned with the fairness of the process," relying on "whether the defendant was probably guilty" instead of the protection

---

[235] Gambell, Suzannah. 217; TerBeek, Calvin. 35.
[236] Gambell, Suzannah. 217.
[237] Clements, Noah. 272.

of his or her constitutional rights.[238] Others argue that allowing "reliable" yet unnecessarily suggestive procedures is "analogous to a Supreme Court ruling that a confession is admissible if it is deemed truthful—regardless of the fact that it had been beaten out of the defendant."[239] Notwithstanding these objections, this discussion is limited to how the standard—and the other case law—increases the risk for misidentification.

Among the five *Biggers* factors, one has no relationship with accuracy ("level of certainty"), two are only related to accuracy in some circumstances ("opportunity... to view the criminal" and "accuracy of the witness's prior description"), and one additional factor has a very limited relationship with accuracy and—in some circumstances—may even have a negative relationship with accuracy ("degree of attention").[240] The factor of certainty, or confidence, is often used as one of the strongest predictors of accuracy, but this belief in some type of confidence-accuracy relationship is "simply outdated and wrong."[241] As discussed earlier in the "Problems with Witness Identifications" section, scientific evidence shows that confidence does not increase accuracy.[242] Instead, confidence is based on "confirmatory feedback" that can be as subtle and immediate as a lineup operator's physical responses or as unavoidable as the eventual confrontation with the identified suspect at trial.[243] This disconnect between accuracy and confidence applies to all types of identifications,

---

[238] Gambell, Suzannah. 214; Gambell, Suzannah. 128 (citing *Manson*, 432 U.S.).

[239] Gambell, Suzannah. [citing Lawrence Taylor, Eyewitness Identification, § 1 (1982)].

[240] The scientific basis from which these conclusions are drawn includes some of the psychological studies discussed in the earlier sections of misidentification, police procedure, and jury decision-making. However, the basis also includes other studies that only become relevant in light of *Biggers'* implied assertion that its five factors are the primary indicators of accuracy. That is, the upcoming section will reference studies from previous sections as well as some new studies that are only now relevant to misidentification.

[241] Gambell, Suzannah. 220; TerBeek, Calvin. 35; In fact, the Vermont Supreme Court recently removed this factor, see footnote 236, supra.

[242] Clements, Noah. 282.

[243] Kolbuchar, Amy, et al. 390.

including cross-racial ones.[244] In spite of this, federal courts are required, and state courts choose, to rely on confidence in determining the reliability of an identification.

What's more, courts rely on confidence even more than they know. This is because confidence has a dangerous "spill-over" effect that gives witnesses an inflated view of the their own experience, including the belief that the lighting was better, that they were "closer to the action," and that the event took longer to occur.[245] This directly impacts witnesses' reports concerning another *Biggers* factor: the "opportunity of the witness to view the criminal." Not only is this retrospective report a function of confidence, but it is also one that witnesses often have a difficult time estimating, especially when it comes to how long they viewed the criminal. While courts interpret viewing time as a proxy for accuracy, a witness's perception of the length of an event is often inaccurate.[246] In one study, subjects estimated that "a time interval of one minute had been anywhere between one second and ten minutes."[247] Additionally, just as traumatic events generally diminish recall, viewing a traumatic crime can distort a witness's recollection of how long it took, usually leading the witness to overestimate the duration.[248] As a result, when courts rely on witness recollection to determine how long the witness viewed the culprit, they are unlikely to receive accurate accounts.

Yet, even if witnesses could accurately remember how long they had an opportunity to view the criminal, there is only a marginal correlation between time observing the perpetrator and accuracy. This is because the length of viewing ceases to be an important determinant of accuracy after a certain length of time, estimated to be somewhere in the range of several minutes.[249] That is, the only study finding

---

[244] Natarajan, Radha. 1841.
[245] Clements, Noah. 281.
[246] Gambell, Suzannah. (citing Arnolds, Edward B., et al. "Eyewitness Testimony: Strategies and Tactics." §2–5, 1984).
[247] Ibid.
[248] Ibid.
[249] Clements, Noah. 280.

marked differences between short and long exposure to an event was a study that compared 10-second exposure times to 30-second exposure times.[250] According to a meta-analysis of 16,000 subjects, comparisons of longer exposure times yield relatively small differences in accuracy.[251] Additionally, the Navy and Marine officer study mentioned earlier yielded the same level of misidentification as other studies with short exposure times, even though the officers were exposed to their interrogators for forty minutes.[252] Therefore, while the "opportunity of the witness to view the criminal" may be correlated with accuracy in some circumstances, the correlation is far less likely to exist when the witness is describing his or her own memory of this "opportunity to view" and when the opportunity is measured only by the length of the viewing. The current *Biggers* factor, as it is listed, makes no mention of this significant caveat, thus creating faith in some identifications where no such faith is warranted.

Another *Biggers* factor that only sometimes correlates with witness reliability is the "accuracy of the witness' prior description of the criminal." This factor fails to correlate with accuracy in cross-racial identifications when the prior description is "race-cumulative."[253] Race-cumulative descriptions are those describing features that, for certain races, do not differentiate between members of that race. This poses a particular threat to black men.[254] While a witness's description of a suspect as having "black hair and dark eyes" may significantly narrow the number of possible white suspects, this description is likely race-cumulative if the witness previously described the culprit as black, as "[these] are not necessarily distinguishing features for a black man."[255] Even though race-cumulative observations "[do] not indicate that the identification is

---

[250] Ibid.
[251] Ibid.
[252] Ibid. 273, 281.
[253] Natarajan, Radha. 1841.
[254] Ibid.
[255] Ibid.

more reliable than if the witness had provided the race alone," courts consistently use such prior descriptions as evidence of witness reliability under this *Biggers* factor, increasing the likelihood that a mistaken cross-racial identification will be allowed to stand, even with the presence of unnecessary suggestiveness.[256]

The fourth *Biggers* factor of concern suggests a link between witness reliability and "the witness's degree of attention." While some measures of attention may positively correlate with accuracy, the most common proxy courts use to measure attention is the stress of the situation, and stress (or trauma) has been shown to have a strong negative correlation with accuracy of facial memory.[257] That is, more stress yields a diminished capacity to remember faces.[258] Justice Blackmun represented the prevailing view at the time when he opined in a 1977 case that stressful situations create a "heightened degree of attention."[259] However, subsequent research proved him wrong, finding that stress, traumatic events, and "weapon focus" all substantially decrease the ability of witnesses to accurately remember faces.[260] Indeed, even those trained to pay attention to faces may be no better at recognizing faces than the general public, as one study found that police officers "specially trained for facial recognition" had the same high rate of misidentification as the control group.[261] In short, while a witness's degree of attention may relate to accuracy in the purest sense, the proxy courts regularly use to measure attention— stress—is negatively related to accuracy, despite common practice and what some on the Court viewed as common sense.

The psychological data invalidates many of the *Biggers* factors in some, if not all, circumstances. Fundamentally, the failure of the

---

[256] Ibid.

[257] Clements, Noah. 281; Gambell, Suzannah. 219.

[258] Clements, Noah. 281.

[259] Gambell, Suzannah. 219; *Moore v. Illinois.* 434 U.S. 220, 1977, 234–235.

[260] Clements, Noah. 273–274; Gambell, Suzannah. 198; Wells, Gary L. "Eyewitness Identification Evidence: Science and Reform." 13; These phenomena were all discussed in previous sections.

[261] Clements, Noah. 281.

Biggers factors revolves around the caveats limiting their applicability. Because the case law includes no standard for determining when to use the factors—and when not to—courts will use these factors even when the given factor has a nonexistent or negative correlation with accuracy.[262] What's more, the *Biggers* standard falls short not only in what it contains but also in what it lacks. Psychological studies on misidentification show that the five listed factors are "under-inclusive," failing to incorporate other post-identification cues that reflect on witness reliability.[263]

Potential factors that *Biggers* left out include the witness's general ability to see well (depth perception, color blindness, visual acuity, etc.), the cross-racial nature of the identification, the pause time before selection during same-race lineup identifications, and the suggestiveness of the identification procedure.[264] These four factors have substantial scientific studies supporting their correlation with accuracy.[265] In fact, the Court in *Manson v. Brathwaite* even referenced one of these lesser-known indicators: the accuracy effect of cross-racial identifications.[266] While the Court certainly did not list cross-racial identifications as another *Biggers* factor, the majority opinion recognized that the identification in the case at hand had a higher likelihood of being accurate because the witness and the defendant were both black.[267] Courts, however, have not chosen to interpret this as a relevant consideration for determining reliability.[268] The same applies to witness sight ability, pre-selection lineup pause time, and procedure suggestiveness.[269]

---

[262] Ibid.
[263] Gambell, Suzannah. 217.
[264] Gambell, Suzannah. 198; Natarajan, Radha. 1828.
[265] Gambell, Suzannah. 198; Natarajan, Radha. 1828.
[266] Natarajan, Radha. 1829.
[267] Ibid. 1828–1829.
[268] Ibid.
[269] Koosed, Margery Malkin. (n 28) 747–748.

What's more, many view the exclusion of this last factor—suggestiveness—as the Court's greatest oversight.[270] Identification reliability is not merely a function of the witness's own statements and experience. It is also affected by police procedures that can taint an individual's memory and substantially increase the chances for misidentification. Psychological studies consistently demonstrated the overwhelming effect of suggestive procedures on witness identification reliability.[271] With suggestibility a factor in the standard, highly-suggestive procedures—like show-ups—would logically create a "higher burden of reliability" from the other factors, just as a witness's limited confidence would create a higher burden under the current standard.[272]

Current application of the *Biggers* standard includes an assessment of whether there was "unnecessary suggestiveness" as a pre-condition for suppressing an identification. However, once unnecessary suggestiveness has been found, the court moves on to the second part of the *Biggers* test, looking at factors supposedly linked to witness reliability, ignoring the procedure's suggestiveness. The "failure to consider the procedure's corrupting effects" in this stage is considered "a serious omission."[273] It has resulted in lower courts allowing "unnecessarily suggestive identifications except in the most outrageous cases," regardless of the extent to which they may have tainted the witness's memory.[274]

The exclusion of procedure suggestiveness—along with the three other previously listed factors substantially affecting

---

[270] Clements, Noah. 281; Gambell, Suzannah. 216; Wells, Gary L. "Eyewitness Identification Evidence: Science and Reform." 19.

[271] Clements, Noah. 273–274; Gambell, Suzannah. 198; Koosed, Margery Malkin. 279; Wells, Gary L. "Eyewitness Identification Evidence: Science and Reform." 13; Wells, Gary L. "Eyewitness Identification: Systemic Reforms." 622; TerBeek, Calvin. 28.

[272] Gambell, Suzannah. 216.

[273] Rosenberg, Benjamin E. "Rethinking the Right to Due Process in Connection with Pretrial Identification Procedures: An Analysis and a Proposal." 79 KY. L. J., 1991, 259, 297.

[274] Gambell, Suzannah. 215.

identification accuracy—prevents *Biggers'* "totality of the circumstances" test from fully measuring witness identification reliability. However, the Court may not have intended this outcome. Specifically, the wording in *Biggers* is unclear as to whether the five factors listed are exhaustive or merely examples.[275] The *Biggers* holding introduces the five factors with these words: "the factors to be considered in evaluating the likelihood of misidentification include…"[276] The use of the word "include" gives the appearance "that the Court meant that the list was not exhaustive."[277] Furthermore, in the *Biggers* decision itself, the Court took into account a factor not listed among the five factors, that the witness did not mistakenly identify other suspects.[278] This consideration, together with the Court's inclusive wording, would indicate a willingness to consider other factors. However, "most lower state and federal courts continue to apply only the five factors given in *Biggers* or add in only one other factor: corroborative evidence of general guilt."[279] Therefore, it seems clear that some of the problems with the *Biggers* standard may be associated with its ambiguity.

Besides the lack of clarity regarding whether the five-factor list is exhaustive, the confusion on a sixth factor of general guilt helps to show the extent to which different interpretations of *Biggers* can yield vastly different results. Moreover, the *Biggers* standard is not the only area of case law where a lack of direction has left fewer protections against misidentification. In the absence of statute or federal case law on the subject, local courts are in the position to grant or (frequently) deny requests for jury instructions and expert testimony on issues that would help juries evaluate witness identifications more effectively.[280] While these are not problems with Supreme Court case law *per se*,

---

[275] Ibid. 217.

[276] Gambell, Suzannah. (citing *Niel v. Biggers*).

[277] Gambell, Suzannah. 217–218.

[278] Gambell, Suzannah. (citing *Niel v. Biggers*).

[279] Gambell, Suzannah. 217.

[280] Gambell, Suzannah. 215; Natarajan, Radha. 1832, 1840.

they are areas where a lack of direction from higher courts and a rigid deference to precedent stand as roadblocks to the in-trial remedies for pre-trial misidentifications.

Jury instructions, as discussed earlier, help jurors to know what they are supposed to consider when in the deliberation room. However, many courts do not allow jury instructions on the issue of misidentification. Radha Natarajan, an attorney, points out some of the main problems of jury instructions as they apply to cross-racial identification cases. The same problems also apply to general cases of misidentification. The courts that do allow some type of instruction usually use the list of *Biggers* factors, suggesting that the jury use these measures to help them determine witness identification reliability.[281] This list of factors obviously encounters the same problems mentioned above: it is under-inclusive and—in some instances—just plain wrong. Even in instances where a witness identification fails *Biggers'* first prong (i.e., it is "unnecessarily suggestive") but passes the second "totality of the circumstances" test, courts rarely permit an instruction on how suggestiveness can taint a witness's identification.[282] Whether the Supreme Court intended this result or not, courts allowing any instruction on potential misidentification usually interpret *Biggers'* five factors as the most appropriate guide to witness reliability.[283]

On an extremely infrequent basis, courts will sometimes deviate from the *Biggers*-as-jury-instruction practice to allow an instruction on cross-racial identifications.[284] However, these instructions invariably fail to state that cross-racial identifications are more susceptible to error, instead simply urging the jury to "consider, if you think it is appropriate to do so, whether the cross-racial nature of

---

[281] Ibid. 1843. See Calcrim No. 315 (California) (though also including "Are the witness and the defendant of different races?")
[282] Ibid. 1843–1844.
[283] Ibid. 1843.
[284] Ibid. 1832, 1844.

the identification has affected the accuracy…"[285] Not only does this vague statement fail to inform jurors of the dangers of cross-racial identification, but it also, ironically, may be counterproductive: studies indicate that some individuals believe cross-racial identifications are more reliable than intra-racial ones.[286] To these individuals, the instruction may seem to buttress that belief.

Another in-trial remedy for pre-trial misidentification is the expert witness who can explain the dangers of misidentification, the correct cues for ascertaining accuracy, and any other studies that are relevant (for example, cross-racial studies). The earlier discussion of expert witnesses pointed out why they are rarely an option for defense attorneys, financially or logistically. However, in the rare circumstances when they are available, courts usually do not permit their testimony.[287] The main reason is precedent, which essentially refers to past practice (and is not necessarily case law in the form of an articulated standard).[288] Courts have not traditionally allowed experts in this field, a determination that made perfect sense before the bulk of the psychological studies were published in the 1980s and 1990s. Now, however, the phenomenon of misidentification is well-documented. Additionally, "[m]ost courts require that expert testimony be in an area outside the jury's province" and, correspondingly, "rule that juries are well aware of the problems inherent in eyewitness identifications."[289] Courts are reluctant to believe that juries need assistance evaluating eyewitnesses who testify, and by using precedent to guide their decisions on this issue, judges frequently rely on cases that were decided before the science of misidentification necessitated experts in the field.[290] Compared to jury instructions and closing arguments

---

[285] Ibid. 1843.
[286] Ibid. 1844.
[287] Ibid. 1833.
[288] Wells, Gary L. "Eyewitness Identification Evidence: Science and Reform." 19.
[289] Natarajan, Radha. 1833.
[290] Natarajan, Radha. 1840–1844; Wells, Gary L. "Eyewitness Identification Evidence: Science and Reform." 18–19.

addressing misidentification dangers, expert testimony on the subject is "allowed the least often by judges."[291]

The lack of clarity in the misidentification case law—either through the vague *Biggers* standard or the lack of guiding principles on the admissibility of jury instructions and experts—means that different courts will use different standards in determining what is presented to the jury at trial. However, the impact of case law extends far beyond the walls of the courtroom, beginning well before even the jury *voir dire*. This is because case law shapes incentives. Specifically, the case law guiding the standards of admissibility and the requirements of due process has a large effect on the types of procedures that police agencies employ. In this regard, the case law changes of *Biggers*, *Brathwaite*, *Kirby*, and *Ash* increase the dangers of misidentification by limiting the responsibility and accountability of the police investigators.

The main impact of the *Biggers* and *Brathwaite* standard has been to clearly establish that unnecessarily suggestive identification procedures are acceptable. As opposed to the earlier *Wade* standard, which informed officers that an unnecessarily suggestive procedure would invariably result in the suppression of the out-of-court identification, unnecessarily suggestive procedures in the post-*Biggers* environment would only be excluded if the defendant could prove a lack of witness reliability based on the five factors. Furthermore, the more investigators knew about the courts' interpretations of *Biggers* over the years, the more freedom they knew they had, as the trial courts generally "use every conceivable method" to avoid suppressing identifications "except in the most outrageous situations."[292]

Investigators, naturally, now have less of an incentive to fastidiously seek out and eliminate the elements of suggestiveness in their identification procedures. Investigators have less of an incentive to avoid inherently suggestive yet convenient procedures, like the

---

[291] Natarajan, Radha. 1844.
[292] Gambell, Suzannah. (citing Grano, Joseph); Grano, Joseph.

66

show-up. And, most of all, investigators have less of an incentive to drastically change lineup procedures to those associated with significantly lower misidentification rates, such as the sequential lineup.[293]

Furthermore, the narrowing of the right to counsel that occurred in *Kirby* and *Ash* freed investigators even more in their execution of pre-indictment and photo lineups. It would be foolhardy to assume that the degree of suggestiveness at lineups is constant and unrelated to the presence of counsel. Therefore, not only do attorneys report suggestiveness and other mistakes to the judge and jury, the very presence of counsel also creates a forceful incentive for the investigating officer to ensure the apparent fairness of the process.[294] This difference in incentives would logically apply equally to pre-indictment and post-indictment lineups, despite the determination in *Kirby* that counsel was only guaranteed at the latter.[295] And as discussed earlier, "all of the problems found in [live] lineups are nearly identical with the issues in photographic lineups or spreads."[296] Therefore, while pre-indictment and photo lineups are as susceptible to suggestiveness and misidentification as post-indictment live lineups, the case law treats them differently, thus removing the lineup administrator's concrete incentive—in the form of an observing attorney—to remain as vigilant against suggestion as possible.

By watering down the requirements for a fair identification procedure, *Biggers*, *Brathwaite*, *Kirby*, and *Ash* not only increase the likelihood that any given "unnecessarily suggestive" identification is presented to the jury, these cases also remove some of the incentives police officers had to avoid these suggestive procedures in the first place. Up to now, however, the discussion has revolved around "likelihoods" and "increased chances" that certain negative results are occurring in the aftermath of these 1970 Supreme Court decisions.

---

[293] Gambell, Suzannah. 216; Kolbuchar, Amy, et al. 397; Mecklenburg, Sheri, et al. 1.
[294] Grano, Joseph. 761; Kolbuchar, Amy, et al. 384.
[295] TerBeek, Calvin. (citing *Kirby v. Illinois*).
[296] TerBeek, Calvin. 29.

Unfortunately, one comprehensive and well-regarded study by University Professors Hugo Bedau and Michael Radelet indicates that there is more to worry about than mere possibilities: witness misidentifications are on the rise.[297] Professors Bedau and Radelet studied "miscarriages of justice," by which they meant convictions of known-to-be innocent defendants. These miscarriages were in 350 "potentially capital crimes," meaning that the crimes were death-eligible in at least one U.S. state.[298] The convictions had occurred from 1900 to 1987 in their first study and extended to 1991 in a follow-up study. While the general purpose of the study was to explore the extent to which capital convictions are subject to error, the study also yielded a large amount of data with which others could analyze trends in the causes for faulty conviction. Upon analyzing the data on eyewitness misidentification, one can see a drastic increase in the rate of misidentification in the 1970s and 1980s.[299] In fact, the rate of eyewitness misidentification after 1970 was double its pre-1970 rate.[300]

In the 1900 to 1987 data set, the rate of proven misidentification among faulty-conviction cases was approximately 16 percent (which is significantly lower than the non-capital misidentification rate because victims—who cannot testify in murder trials—are the most common eyewitnesses in all other cases). However, the sixty-four post-1970 miscarriages of justice were

---

[297] Bedau, Hugo and Michael L. Radelet. "Miscarriages of Justice in Potentially Capital Cases." Stanford Law Review, vol. 40, 1987, 21; Koosed, Margery Malkin. 274 (citing Bedau, Hugo and Michael L. Radelet).

[298] Bedau, Hugo and Michael L. Radelet. 21; Koosed, Margery Malkin. 274 (citing Bedau, Hugo and Michael L. Radelet); Radelet, Michael L., et al. "In Spite of Innocence: Erroneous Convictions in Capital Cases." Northeastern, 1992.

[299] Bedau, Hugo and Michael L. Radelet. 57, 179; Koosed, Margery Malkin. 275 (citing Bedau, Hugo and Michael L. Radelet). I am citing the Koosed article because that article made me generally aware of this data and the implications. However, I wanted to use different years in my analysis and, therefore, sought the data source myself. Page 179 of the Bedau and Radelet work is the appendix that includes the relevant dates.

[300] Bedau, Hugo and Michael L. Radelet. 57, 179.

attributed to mistaken identification in 28 percent of the cases while the pre-1970 miscarriages had a 13 percent misidentification rate.[301] An even higher rate applies when considering the 1987 to 1991 data in their second study.[302]

Although some possible alternative explanations can be made, they seem highly unlikely. This rise in known misidentifications leading to faulty convictions could be because eyewitness error is now more documented than it was before. However, Law Professor Margery Koosed points out that the observed rise is comparative to other sources of faulty conviction, and there is no data indicating that cases of eyewitness identification would be more documented than other causes of error.[303] Another possible explanation is that courts may be more sensitive to the problem. Yet, with the high burdens the *Biggers* rule places on the defense and the unlikelihood of exclusion, compared to other sources of conviction, "there is little added incentive for the courts or counsel to look for these [misidentification] mistakes, particularly after-conviction."[304]

The most reasonable interpretation of Professors Bedau and Radelet's data is that misidentifications are on the rise.[305] And at least for the most dangerous type of cases—those that are "death eligible" so a defendant's life could be on the line—the post-1970 rate is double the previous one. The state of case law may be a significant cause of this rise, with *Biggers*'s over- and under-inclusiveness, the lack of clarity and guidance, and the modified incentives all fostering procedures that lead to misidentification. But case law alone cannot be

---

[301] Bedau, Hugo and Michael L. Radelet. 179. I arrived at these calculations by reviewing the appendix and counting the total number of "miscarriages" and the total number of miscarriages associated with accidental witness misidentification, and then finding both sets of numbers for the pre-1970 data and the post-1979 data. Dividing the misidentification miscarriages by the total miscarriages yielded the number of cases for each period for which misidentification was a cause of faulty conviction.

[302] Koosed, Margery Malkin. 285 (citing Radelet, Michael L., et al.).

[303] Koosed, Margery Malkin. 286.

[304] Ibid.

[305] Ibid.

the source of all faulty convictions that are based on misidentifications. As a previously discussed meta-analysis concluded, as much as one half to two thirds of all faulty convictions are based on eyewitness misidentification.[306] The dilemma's scope makes any single source seem insufficient and unlikely to account for more than a fraction of the problem.

Indeed, eyewitness misidentification arises because of a confluence of factors that build upon each other. Psychological principles, police procedures, cross-racial dangers, jury unawareness, and binding case law all combine to endanger the liberty of innocent suspects. When examined separately, these issues create concern. When examined together, however, they establish the dire need for systematic reform. The problems with case law, therefore, are simply the final straw, showing how the criminal justice system urgently needs reforms that will address the danger of eyewitness misidentification.

---

[306] Clements, Noah. 275.

Chapter 4

REFORM

Substantially reducing misidentifications will require significant reforms. Indeed, the problem's multifaceted nature necessitates a comprehensive response. Several aspects of the identification and in-trial procedures must change to decrease the likelihood of eyewitness misidentification and equip juries for seeing the dangers and relevant cues associated with misidentifications. This chapter will argue for eight police- and trial-level reforms and explain why other suggested reforms are impractical or ill-advised.

After the explanation of the eight relevant reforms, however, an analysis of the progress of reform will show that none of the possible solutions have been implemented on a wide scale—despite the fact that some have been urged for decades. An analysis of this failure and its causes will demonstrate that the current mechanism for implementation is piecemeal and insufficient. This will lead to the final policy recommendation that state law must mandate these eight procedural changes to ensure implementation and consistency.

Chapter 4.1: Eight Reforms

The eight reforms presented here would change police procedure and courtroom practice without infringing on the interest of law enforcement. They would address the main psychological and practical problems that lead to misidentification and subsequent faulty conviction. These reforms are, very briefly, (1) sequential lineups with limited "laps," (2) double-blind administration of lineups, (3) modified lineup instructions, (4) the use of technology to replace show-ups, (5) changes in lineup composition, (6) immediate measures of witness confidence and observation details, (7) the general statutory allowance of misidentification experts at trial, and (8) extensive jury instructions on misidentifications and proper accuracy cues. These eight general reforms each have subsections, which make up a total of just over twenty specific proposals. Table 2, below, lists the main misidentification problems and how the general eight suggested solutions correspond to those problems.

TABLE 2

Misidentification Problems and Their Corresponding Solutions

Problem	Solution
RELATIVE JUDGMENT	#1 Sequential lineups with limited laps
SUGGESTIVENESS (on the part of the lineup administrator)	#2 Double-blind administration
SUGGESTIVENESS (implied in the lineup procedure)	#3 Modified Lineup Instructions
SUGGESTIVENESS (inherent in show-ups)	#4 Replacement of Show-ups
MEMORY WEAKNESS (general)	#5 Lineup Composition Changes (#4 Replacement of Show-ups)*
FEEDBACK'S EFFECTS	#6 Immediate Measures of Confidence & Observation Details (#2 Double-blind administration)
JURY KNOWLEDGE	#7 Experts #8 Jury Instructions
CASE LAW (lack of clarity, insufficient incentives, and the failure of *Biggers*)	(underlying issues remedied by the eight reforms)

*The solutions in parenthesis are those that have already been listed.

The reforms I propose here are partly based on past suggested reforms. However, in specifics, scope, and suggested implementation, this set of eight reforms differs significantly from any past recommendations. First, several of the reforms outlined here have either never been suggested or have only been advanced to combat one aspect of a problem. Specifically, the suggestion of the complete

72

replacement of show-ups with computerized lineups (reform #4), the insistence on forbidding excessive sequential lineup "laps" (reform #1, part B), and the recommendation for a full set of general and race-specific jury instructions (reform #8) that will be outlined below, which are to be created directly through state law, are all recommendations that are new to the body of misidentification reform literature.

Furthermore, excluding Ms. Natarajan's recent article on cross-racial issues, few scholars on misidentification seem to pay much attention to the dangers of cross-racial identification. This may be partly because the recommendations would make the situation worse, as they place too high a burden on law enforcement (in the requirement of substantial corroboration) or take necessary power away from the jury (by having the judge determine reliability). It makes sense, then, that none of the proposals (before or after Ms. Natarajan's meta-analysis) devote space to tailoring their recommendations to the lessons and issues that cross-racial studies have shown. General and widely accepted misidentification reform proposals, which often include Reforms #1, #2, #3, and #5, fail to recognize the differences and unique dangers of cross-racial identifications. With an eye towards these dangers, I have incorporated them into the recommendations listed here (specifically, in reforms #5, #6C, #7B, and #8B).

Another area in which my recommendations differ from the current literature lies in my belief that, besides decreasing the likelihood of misidentification, we must also decrease the likelihood that misidentifications—should they occur—will result in faulty convictions. While some state commissions and other reputable national organizations have advocated for specific changes to police procedure to combat misidentification, none of the proposed reforms take the necessary two-part approach to reducing wrongful convictions based on faulty identifications. Specifically, the major reform proposals fail to create in-trial protections (like jury instructions) for innocent suspects who—despite new, non-suggestive police

73

procedure—are still in danger of being misidentified. These major reform proposals, which dominate the discourse on the matter, seem to show a naïve belief that remedying the dangers of police procedure is enough to remove the danger of misidentification-based false conviction. However, as demonstrated in General Psychological Studies and Principles presented in Chapter 2.1, police procedure is just one part of the problem; thus, the correction of faulty procedures is only one part of a solution. The recommendations for state law allowing the use of expert witnesses (reform #7A), expanding the scope of expert testimony (reform #7B), and providing explicit jury instructions on misidentifications (reform #8) all address what must be a necessary second part of any effort to fully and comprehensively combat the danger of wrongful conviction based on misidentification.

Finally, as I will explain in further depth after presenting these reforms, past efforts at reform have failed because they are presented as "recommendations" and "new suggested guidelines," without being forced upon law enforcement agencies and written into the law. This is often because the recommending organizations (national organizations, non-binding commissions, or federal agencies) have no control over local and state law enforcement. Local discretion and a reliance on state commission recommendations have resulted in a piecemeal, incomplete, dangerously slow implementation of even the most widely accepted reform ideas, four of which are suggested here.

In decreasing misidentifications, the means of implementation is as important a step as the specifics of the reforms. Therefore, while my final recommendation of a state law (mandating the use of these eight practices) may be at odds with the tenor and nature of past reforms, it is a necessary step any state must take if it wants to protect innocent suspects—in any significant way—from the dangers of misidentification.

Chapter 4.2: Rejected Reforms:

Before going directly into the eight reforms, it would be useful to examine very briefly a few other prominent reform ideas that would unduly burden or distort the criminal justice system. Most of these reforms are from authors and scholars whose underlying data I used for my analysis but whose conclusions I reject as unacceptable. These reforms regard overarching solutions, radical changes to police procedure, or changes to trial procedure that would distort the criminal justice system.

Most of the overarching "solutions" involve placing onerous burdens on investigators and prosecutors. One author whose article appeared in the Indiana Law Review suggests eliminating all witness testimony from criminal trials unless the witness is familiar with the suspect.[307] Another critic of current practice, a distinguished misidentification expert and professor of psychology from Iowa State University, suggests that all witness testimony should be corroborated by a "substantial" amount of other evidence or another witness.[308] This proposal, however, seems no more logical than allowing a "sixth" *Biggers* factor of corroborating evidence; no amount of corroboration can make an identification reliable. What's more, corroboration does not have any direct relation to an eyewitness's reliability. These logical disconnects—along with the fact that the eight reforms presented below will increase the accuracy and juror knowledge of identifications—make a requirement for corroboration unnecessarily burdensome for law enforcement.

Other reformers suggest that police officers should be forced to acquire a warrant to conduct a lineup with a suspect or the suspect's photograph and that judges should only grant such warrants when presented with some type of "reasonable suspicion" of guilt.[309] However, while warrants may be required for an invasion of one's

---

[307] Clements, Noah. 287.
[308] Wells, Gary L. "Eyewitness Identification: Systemic Reforms."
[309] Ibid.

privacy or a potentially damaging act, the overarching qualm with identification procedures resides in the danger that they may facilitate misidentification. This is especially true given the presumably lower level of "reasonable suspicion" that would be applied in deciding whether to issue a warrant. Thus, requiring a warrant not only burdens law enforcement but also does absolutely nothing to diminish the danger of misidentification once a lineup has been authorized.

Finally, several other authors suggest reforms that would take the decision-making power away from jurors, giving judges the authority to "throw out" certain identifications either before trial or in the appeal stage.[310] Ms. Natarajan, for example, argues that judges should evaluate the accuracy of an identification—regardless of whether it was "unnecessarily suggestive"—and only allow testimony from eyewitnesses that are determined to be reliable.[311] Attorney Calvin TerBeek, writing for the Law and Psychology Review, similarly argues that in all cases where the evidence of guilt is solely an eyewitness identification, appellate courts should "engage in a *de novo* review of the facts and circumstances surrounding the eyewitness," which means that the appellate court would effectively hold a new trial, ignoring the jury verdict and, as the author admits, virtually "eliminating jury trials" in these types of cases.[312] However, these radical changes undermine the fundamental purpose of the jury: to weigh the facts of the case. "It is part of our adversary system that we accept at trial much evidence that has strong elements of untrustworthiness,"[313] and the jury is the body to determine what is

---

[310] Natarajan, Radha. 1839.

[311] Ibid. The Supreme Court of Maine held that an unreliable identification may not be considered "relevant" evidence, and/or "competent" testimony; the court, pursuant to its "gatekeeping function," may be "required to examine the witness's identification testimony to ensure that it was relevant and competent." *State v. Davis*, 191 A. 3d 1147 (2018). See footnote 216, supra, at fn. 75.

The New Jersey Supreme Court has similarly required a judge "to determine the admissibility of the identification evidence." See *State v. Chen*, 27 A. 3d 930 (2011).

[312] TerBeek, Calvin. 48.

[313] Clements, Noah. 284 (citing *Mason v. Brathwaite*, 432 U.S. 98, 113 n. 14 (1977) [quoting *Clemons v. United States*, 408 F.2d 1230, 1251 (D.C. Circuit 1968)]).

and is not trustworthy. Since this proper weighing can only occur with fair procedures and a properly informed jury, the eight reforms presented below decrease the danger of misidentification while still preserving the jury system.

Chapter 4.3: Explanation of Tier-One Reforms (One Through Six)

The following subsections discuss the first six reforms that are necessary to balance the interests of law enforcement with the need to reduce the danger of misidentification. Each section will provide a brief summary of the most relevant facts discussed in the previous sections, orienting the reader to the specific link between the evidence and the proposed reform. The sections will also discuss whether the reform has been suggested before, identify whether the reform has ever been implemented, and present a succinct delineation of the reform's exact subsidiary parts.

Reform #1: Sequential Lineups

Universal use of sequential instead of simultaneous lineups would reduce the rate of misidentification by preventing witnesses from employing relative judgment in making their decisions. As mentioned earlier, sequential lineups occur when officers show witnesses photographs or live suspects one at a time and, for each, ask the witness whether or not that individual is the perpetrator.

Many psychologists are convinced that the sequential lineup is one of the most important steps in reducing the risk of misidentification. [314] Indeed, several studies of the sequential method found that—when coupled with the next recommendation of double-blind administration—it reduced the rate of misidentification by more than 50 percent. [315] Perhaps more importantly, this substantial reduction in misidentification occurred without a notable reduction in

---

[314] Clements, Noah. 287.
[315] Ibid.

the rate of correct identification.[316] There was only a 1 percent reduction in correct identifications, most likely due to more cautious witnesses. [317]

The success of the sequential lineup is attributed to its reduction of relative judgment.[318] Witnesses know that other pictures are coming and that these pictures may more effectively remind them of the culprit. As a result, with each picture, witnesses are "forced to dig a bit more deeply into memory" to make an identification.[319] For sequential lineups to avoid relative judgment for the entire sequence of photos, witnesses must not know how many photos they will be shown or which photo is the last in the series.[320]

The overwhelming scientific and experimental data on the subject demonstrates the advantages of sequential lineups.[321] Sequential lineups reduce the rate of misidentifications without substantially decreasing the rate of correct identifications.[322] The U.S. Department of Justice, several state commissions, and a number of

---

[316] Ibid.; Wells, Gary L. "Eyewitness Identification: Systemic Reforms." 627.

[317] Wells, Gary L. "Eyewitness Identification: Systemic Reforms." 627.

[318] Kolbuchar, Amy, et al. 388.

[319] Ibid. 395.

[320] Wells, Gary L. "Eyewitness Identification: Systemic Reforms." 626.

[321] Clements, Noah. 287; Kolbuchar, Amy, et al. 388; Wells, Gary L. "Eyewitness Identification: Systemic Reforms." 627. While an Illinois pilot project resulted in a rate of filler identification that was higher for sequential lineups compared to simultaneous lineups, the implementation of the pilot project was faulty, as numerous studies have noted, including Schacter, D., et al. "Studying eyewitness investigations in the field." *Law and Human Behavior*, 2007, and O'Toole, T. P. "What's the matter with Illinois? How an opportunity was squandered to conduct an important study on eyewitness identification procedures." *Champion*, 2006, 18–23. Specifically, there were concerns of "biased lineup structure," "poorly matched fillers," and "suggestive lineup procedures" in the non-sequential, non-blind procedure, thus decreasing the rate of filler identification. Because the study compared sequential *double-blind* lineups to simultaneous non-blind lineups, it was impossible to distinguish between the two effects. Furthermore, filler identification is not an appropriate measure of misidentification rates if biased instructions or procedures directed witnesses towards certain suspects, which would reduce the rate of filler identification without reducing the "dangerous error rate."

[322] Clements, Noah. 287; Wells, Gary L. "Eyewitness Identification: Systemic Reforms." 627.

advocacy organizations have recommended that local police agencies adopt sequential lineups, although only a limited number of have required sequential lineups, such as the states of New Jersey and North Carolina, which have required sequential lineup "whenever possible."[323] And while at least one jurisdiction switching to the sequential lineup procedure noted concerns with the early stages of implementation—including concerns regarding the manpower required to set up the photo sequences—"ultimately, this change in the lineup procedure caused few problems, none of them serious or enduring."[324]

The sequential lineup procedure promises to help reduce the rate of misidentification. However, as noted in the "Police Procedure" section of Chapter 2, those jurisdictions using sequential lineups also allow laps, whereby witnesses can request to go through the photos numerous times and resort to relative judgments.[325] While the filler identification rate in a purely sequential lineup is approximately 3 percent, for two, three, or more laps the rate goes up to 10, 14, and 75 percent, respectively.[326] Nonetheless, virtually no police agencies have been willing to adopt sequential lineups unless some use of laps is allowed.[327] Therefore, if laps are to be allowed, the laps must be limited in number—preferably to two additional laps—as the rate of error is considerably higher for witnesses who need more than two laps.

While some other explanations of sequential laps indicate that officers should urge the eyewitness to limit the number of laps, I feel that this numerical limit must be set regardless of the witness's request. The use of laps should also be recorded for possible use at trial, a practice some police departments employ.[328] Additionally, juries must be made to understand that a witness's need to see the photos again

---

[323] Collins, Winn S. "Safeguards for Eyewitness Identification." *Wisconsin Lawyer*, March 2004, 11; TerBeek, Calvin. 47.
[324] Kolbuchar, Amy, et al. 405–406.
[325] Wells, Gary L. "Eyewitness Identification: Systemic Reforms." 627–628.
[326] Kolbuchar, Amy, et al. 397–398.
[327] Wells, Gary L. "Eyewitness Identification: Systemic Reforms." 628.
[328] Ibid. 627–628.

reflects a relative weakness in the witness's memory and, therefore, reflects an increased likelihood of error. No current reform institutionalizes a way of informing the jury that subsequent laps signify memory weakness. I believe that this last aim is best accomplished through a jury instruction informing jurors of what it means for a witness to fail to identify a suspect on the first lap. In short, if laps are to be used, they must be minimized, recorded, and explained.

This leads to the following policy recommendations:

REFORM #1: Sequential Lineups

1A. Police agencies should use sequential instead of simultaneous lineups.[329]

1B. Police agencies should not allow subsequent laps for sequential lineups.

1C. In the event that police agencies allow subsequent laps:

I. laps should be limited in number, preferably to a maximum of two additional laps,

II. the use of additional laps should be recorded, and

III. state law should provide for a jury instruction that informs jurors of how many laps occurred and the significance of a witness's failure to identify a suspect in the first sequential lineup lap.

---

[329] The New Jersey caveat—that police agencies employ sequential lineups "whenever possible"—may have been included more for political tenability than for any other meaningful reason. Once police agencies make the simple transition from photo boards to photo cards, sequential lineups are always "possible." Additionally, sequential live lineups merely involve the police officer showing the lineup members behind viewing glass one at a time. While a caveat of this nature may be meaningful in a different type of recommendation, it is not here if one is to assume that transition time will be provided to all agencies required to move to sequential lineups.

Reform #2: Double-Blind Administration of Lineups

Suggestiveness plays a large role in facilitating misidentifications.[330] Like all the psychological, procedural, and case-law-related problems, the dangers of suggestiveness have been reviewed in earlier sections, and they come in the form of officer action and procedural characteristics. The "vast scientific literature" clearly demonstrates that the "double-blind administration" of lineups is the only way to effectively and practically eliminate the subtle, frequently unintentional effects of officer suggestion.[331] Double-blind administration refers to a condition that the lineup administrator be "blind" to the identity of the suspect. That is, unlike the custom in regular lineups, the administrating officer does not know who the police are suspecting and, therefore, is less likely to employ suggestive practices.

The need for double-blind lineup administration is "merely an acknowledgement that people in law enforcement, like people in behavior and medical research, are influenced by their own beliefs and unknowingly 'leak' this information, both verbally and nonverbally, in ways that can influence the person being tested."[332] As mentioned above, double-blind testing reduces misidentifications by over 50 percent when combined with sequential lineups.[333] Furthermore, studies in a number of different fields have established that double-blind testing is crucial when there is face-to-face contact between the tester and the subject.[334] Double-blind testing is particularly important in pre-indictment and photo lineups, when suspects and defendants are not afforded the right to the presence of their lawyer, who could otherwise watch for suggestiveness.[335]

---

[330] Steblay, Nancy K. Mehrkens. 347; TerBeek, Calvin. 28–29.
[331] Wells, Gary L. "Eyewitness Identification: Systemic Reforms." 629.
[332] Ibid.
[333] Clements, Noah. 287.
[334] Wells, Gary L. "Eyewitness Identification: Systemic Reforms." 629.
[335] Ibid. See also footnote 192, supra.

Double-blind administration is necessary for another reason beyond the need to remove pre-identification suggestiveness. The procedure is also required to decrease the enormous possibility of feedback to the witness after identification.[336] The investigator's immediate response—verbal and nonverbal—influences the witness's report of confidence and the details of the initial incident. Any feedback can "cement false memories and erase any original uncertainty" on the part of the witness.[337] Part and parcel with this aim is the requirement that witnesses know of their investigator's ignorance. If witnesses are told that their investigator does not know the identity of the suspect, they will be less likely to "seek or infer cues from the officer's behavior," both before and after the identification.[338]

Many police departments that are using sequential lineups are also using double-blind administration.[339] These include a growing number of states, starting with New Jersey and continuing to a significant number of jurisdictions or states.[340] The State of California has enacted comprehensive legislation for "photo lineups and live lineups," which includes, "The investigator conducting the identification procedure shall use blind administration or blinded administration during the identification procedure."[341] As with the sequential lineup procedure, several organizations and states are advocating double-blind lineups, including the U.S. Department of

---

[336] Wells, Gary L. "Eyewitness Identification: Systemic Reforms." 630.
[337] Ibid.
[338] Kolbuchar, Amy, et al. 389.
[339] TerBeek, Calvin. 47.
[340] Collins, Winn S. 11; Kolbuchar, Amy, et al. 406; https://www.cga.ct.gov/jud/tfs/20130901_Eyewitness%20Identification%20Task%20Force/20111019/Jurisdictions%20That%20Use%20Double-Blind%20Sequential%20Presentation%20of%20Lineups.pdf, September 11, 2011, accessed on September 1, 2019; https://www.innocenceproject.org/eyewitness-identification-reform/, accessed on September 1, 2019.
[341] California Penal Code § 859.7 (2018).

Justice.[342] Still, police agencies have expressed some concerns with double-blind lineups. These mostly regard manpower and witness-investigator rapport.[343]

Some police agencies, particularly smaller departments, worry that they will be short-staffed if officers and other law enforcement officials have to spend time as lineup administrators in cases with which they are not involved.[344] This is particularly a concern when, in big cases, the entire police force may be working on the same case, making it hard to find someone who does not know who the suspect is. The same applies to cases with several eyewitnesses: one eyewitness's stated confidence in a certain lineup member's guilt may make the officer no longer "blind" for the purposes of subsequent witnesses.[345] There is also the worry that uninvolved lineup administrators do not have the same established rapport that a crime investigator may have developed with the witness over the course of an investigation. These concerns have served as a roadblock to the implementation of double-blind lineup administration in some police agencies.[346]

Despite these fears, most agencies that have begun employing double-blind administration "were able to overcome most issues with minimal difficulty."[347] For example, one department used officers from the property crime division to serve as blind administrators in the crimes against persons division, and vice versa. Also, some agencies are considering the use of replicable computer programs that administer sequential photo lineups, which witnesses can operate out of the sight of investigators.[348]

In short, implementation concerns have mostly been unfounded, and agencies have been able to successfully employ double-blind

---

[342] Clements, Noah. 287; Kolbuchar, Amy, et al. 388; Wells, Gary L. "Eyewitness Identification: Systemic Reforms." 627.
[343] Kolbuchar, Amy, et al. 407.
[344] Ibid. 406–407.
[345] Ibid. 407.
[346] Ibid.
[347] Ibid. 406–407.
[348] Ibid. 406.

lineups without notable difficulties. Furthermore, the minor difficulties that some agencies may encounter are a small price to pay when weighed against the considerable dangers of officer suggestiveness.

This leads to the following policy recommendations:

REFORM #2: Double-Blind Administration of Lineups

> **2A:** Lineup administrators should not be aware of which lineup member is the suspect.

> **2B:** Witnesses should be informed that lineup administrators do not know which lineup member is the suspect.

> **2C:** Police agencies should be encouraged to use computerized photo lineups if double-blind lineup administration would be inconvenient.[349]

Reform #3: Modified Lineup Instructions

While double-blind lineup administration can virtually eliminate officer suggestiveness, it does nothing to remove aspects of suggestion that are inherent in any lineup. Specifically, witnesses may assume that the use of a lineup signifies that the police have apprehended the culprit and that the culprit is present in the lineup. As discussed in the police procedure section, psychological studies show that these assumptions regularly occur and increase the rate of misidentification.[350] To remedy this, police officers must instruct witnesses otherwise, explicitly telling them that the culprit may be absent.

Several studies of pre-identification lineup instructions to this effect found the instructions to lower the misidentification rate when

---

[349] Computerized photo lineups are discussed in further depth in the description of Reform #4: Computerized Photo Lineups to Replace Show-ups.
[350] Steblay, Nancy K. Mehrkens. 344.

the culprit was not in the lineup.[351] After receiving these instructions, eyewitnesses were far less likely to choose any of the lineup members in these culprit-absent lineups. Moreover, these studies found no difference in the willingness to choose a lineup member in the culprit-present lineups. Thus, lineup instructions warning the witness of the real culprit's possible absence decrease the rate of misidentification without decreasing the rate of accurate identification.[352]

Proper lineup instructions remind the witness that "it is just as important to clear innocent persons from suspicion as to identify guilty parties," and the U.S. Department of Justice has recommended a lineup instruction to this effect—in addition to recommending an instruction on the possible absence of the real culprit.[353]

Nonetheless, this necessary reform and the five that will follow have all received comparatively little or no attention in light of many advocates' apparent belief that double-blind, sequential lineups can serve as a panacea for misidentification.[354] For example, in spite of the psychological evidence showing the need for such instructions, the Boston Police Commissioner's 2004 Task-Force Recommendations for Eyewitness Identification, which was considered "the new gold standard" for eyewitness identification procedure, fails to even mention instructions of the type discussed here.[355] Still, some commissions and advocacy organizations have urged this type of lineup instruction change, with New Jersey requiring it in all jurisdictions.[356] California similarly requires that the eyewitness be

---

[351] Steblay, Nancy M. "Social Influence in Eyewitness Recall: A Meta-Analytic Review of Lineup Instruction Effects." Law and Human Behavior, vol. 21, no. 3, 1997, 283, 285–86; Wells, Gary L. "Eyewitness Identification: Systemic Reforms." 625.

[352] Wells, Gary L. "Eyewitness Identification: Systemic Reforms." 625.

[353] Steblay, Nancy K. Mehrkens. 348

[354] Collins, Winn S. 11; Kolbuchar, Amy, et al. 395.

[355] "Task Force Recommendations on Eyewitness Identification." *Prosecutor*, National District Attorneys Association, March/April 2005, 16.

[356] Farmer, John (New Jersey Attorney General). "Attorney General Guidelines for Preparing and Conducting Photo and Live Lineup Identification Procedures." Public Letter, April 18, 2001.

instructed that "The perpetrator may or may not be among the persons in the identification procedure."[357]

One possible reason for the limited attention given to pre-identification instructions may be counter-intuitive: their implementation is too easy. The use of sequential, double-blind lineups takes considerable effort, as it involves a near-complete overhaul of the lineup process. This difficulty—along with its associated gains in fighting misidentification—seems to have directed much reform energy towards the fight for sequential, double-blind procedures.[358] Smaller, simpler reforms, including the creation of this suggested lineup instruction, have received far less attention. But the size of a reform does not always correspond to the size of its impact. And failing to forcefully advocate for lineup instructions because they are commonsensical and easy to implement can mean that they will be overlooked, especially by departments that are unwilling to overhaul their lineup process and mistakenly perceive all eyewitness procedure reform as one big package.

Neither of the two previously listed reforms nor any of the subsequent five is able to address the danger of inherent lineup suggestiveness. Therefore, regardless of whatever other efforts are being made, lineup administrators must inform the witness that the culprit may not be in the lineup.

This leads to the following policy recommendation:

REFORM #3: Modified Lineup Instructions

> Witnesses should be informed that the culprit may not be present in the lineup.

Reform #4: Computerized Photo Lineups to Replace Show-ups

Of all the identification procedures used, show-ups are by far the most prone to misidentification. They are the "most grossly suggestive"

---

[357] California Penal Code § 859.7(a)(4)(A) (2018).
[358] Collins, Winn S. 11.

procedure ever used by police, and they fail to sufficiently test witnesses' memories.[359] When witnesses make identifications in show-ups, the likelihood of error is estimated to be around 15 percent.[360] Unlike lineups, when the rate of general error is split among the suspect and five fillers, all show-up error is "dangerous error," indicating that it implicates the innocent individual whom police officers already suspect to be the culprit.[361]

Notwithstanding these problems, show-ups have a number of advantages, mostly revolving around their immediate nature. In a time-sensitive investigation—as most are—show-ups allow police to take immediate action that could lead to the apprehension of the criminal or the speedy continued pursuit of other suspects. Therefore, it may be ill-advised to prohibit the use of show-ups without some way of retaining the advantages of immediate notification.

Among the reform ideas that have been examined, all those mentioning show-ups essentially suggest that police departments avoid these show-ups whenever possible. However, one feasible way to permanently eliminate the show-up would be to replace it with computerized photo lineups that officers could present to eyewitnesses on laptops or similar devices. Computerized photo lineups have been in existence—if not widespread use—for the past several years.[362] The computers cycle through a series of pictures, giving the informational prompts that an investigator might. "Computer-based imaging systems" currently exist for station-house lineups, and my assessment of this relatively simple technology—along with confirmatory feedback regarding feasibility from attorneys with the New Jersey Public Defender's office and the Contra Costa County, California, District Attorney's office—clearly indicates that minor modifications to the pool of "filler" stock photos would allow the program to be used

---

[359] Gambell, Suzannah. 193.

[360] Steblay, Nancy K. Mehrkens. 353.

[361] Ibid.

[362] Crimestar. "Law Enforcement Record Management and Investigation System." http://www.crimestar.com/lineups.html, accessed on April 1, 2008.

at the scene of a crime based on a digital photograph of the suspect.[363] With sufficient lighting and a portable, headshot-sized white paper backing, the suspect's photo would look similar enough to the stock photos, especially if the pool of stock photos is slightly varied in lighting and has a background shade of white.[364] By using a photo of an on-the-scene suspect, incorporated into a digital lineup on a police laptop or PDA, the identification can have all the advantages of timeliness without placing the suspect at such a grave risk of being misidentified.

Granted, this proposal would be expensive. Unlike the other seven proposals presented here—which require no maintenance and have nominal setup costs—this proposal would require any given police department to purchase a digital camera and a laptop (or smartphone) if they do not already have one. Therefore, any requirement on this transition from show-ups to computerized photo displays would have to come with money from the state. A rough estimate of this one-time cost comes to about $61,600 for a state of 10 million people.[365] However, even if the expenditure were ten times this

---

[363] Personal communications with Joseph Krakora, Deputy Public Defender, New Jersey, and Gary Koepell, Deputy District Attorney, Contra Costa County, California.
[364] Ibid.; Personal communications with Joshua Parker, Attorney, New York.
[365] This estimate is based on a number of statistics on police agencies and the incidence of crimes involving the need for a show-up. In order to err on the side of caution, this cost estimate assumed that no police agencies had laptops or digital cameras. This is highly unlikely given the fact that the U.S. Department of Justice's Bureau of Statistics estimates that 83 percent of police officers worked for an agency that used in-field computers. This assumption also assumed that one out of every ten crimes involving eyewitnesses (estimated at 154,000 per year through the figures in Wells, Gary L. "Eyewitness Identification Evidence: Science and Reform." 19). The per-item price estimates for digital cameras and laptops was $200 and $1000, respectively. Finally, the frequency of necessary show-ups was estimated to be about 10 percent of eyewitness cases (based on personal communication with Attorney Joshua Parker). Thus, 154,000 crimes with eyewitnesses, divided by 10 for the 10 percent necessary show-up rate, times $1200 for the laptop and digital camera, divided by 10 for the estimated necessity of only one laptop and camera per ten show-ups, yields $1,848,000 for all the show-ups in any given year in the United States. Assuming that cases involving eyewitnesses are relatively proportional to the population of the U.S., that yields $6,160 per million residents. Thus, the one-time

amount, it would be a small (one-time) price to pay in order to substantially decrease the risk of misidentification.

This leads to the following policy recommendations:

REFORM #4: Computerized Photo Lineups to Replace Show-ups

4A: States should provide funding to assure that every police agency has the equipment to provide on-the-scene digital lineups to witnesses.

4B: Police agencies should be prohibited from using show-ups and, instead, should perform on-the-scene computerized photo lineups when immediacy is particularly important.

---

cost to update a state's police agencies with digital cameras and some laptops might be $61,600 for a state of 10 million people. While this estimate is extremely rough, it gives a general idea of how much such an upgrade might cost. Furthermore, regardless of that cost of equipment and the number of "necessary show-up" instances in a given jurisdiction, police agencies already equipped with laptops and digital cameras will likely not need additional state funding.

Reform #5: Lineup Composition Changes

The past four reforms involve changes to the standard practices at the vast majority of police departments. In the area of lineup composition, most police agencies select the lineup members in ways that minimize misidentifications. However, some agencies set up lineups in ways that exacerbate witness mistakes. Even in many of the jurisdictions that have lineup composition standards, officers have no statutory obligation to comply with these standards.[366] In order for lineups to serve their purpose, lineup administrators must make sure that lineups are sufficient tests of memory, splitting the general error rate over as many "appropriate" fillers as possible. Additionally, the officers must make photo records of the lineup available to defense counsel.

In terms of ensuring that the lineups are sufficient tests of memory, lineup administrators should have at least five fillers, which is the standard practice.[367] And because using more fillers in photo lineups involves almost no additional cost, these lineups should have even more members (assuming the suspect is still only shown next to photos of similar-looking individuals). In no instance should the suspect stand out from the lineup members, as this increases the chance that the witness will be "drawn" towards that lineup member.[368] If the suspect has unique features that would make the suspect invariably stand out in a live lineup (when the police officers have access to a particularly limited pool of individuals who can serve as fillers), the suspect should be presented in a photo lineup. For example, if a suspect is of Chinese descent and the police department does not have enough Chinese-American officers or inmates to have five fillers, they should use a photo lineup, which would ostensibly have stock photos of Chinese fillers. New Jersey has a procedural requirement to this effect, although it merely suggests that the suspect

---

[366] TerBeek, Calvin. 47; Wells, Gary L. "Eyewitness Identification: Systemic Reforms." 641.
[367] Steblay, Nancy K. Mehrkens. 352.
[368] Wells, Gary L. "Eyewitness Identification: Systemic Reforms." 641.

not "unduly" stand out and notes that "complete uniformity of features is not required."[369] California also requires that the suspect "not unduly stand out."[370]

Furthermore, Ms. Natarajan coined the term "race cumulative" to refer to features that describe an entire race and, therefore, do not differentiate between members of that race.[371] She brought up this point to suggest that one of *Biggers'* totality of the circumstances factors, "accuracy of... prior description," excludes descriptions that are "race cumulative."[372] However, I believe that a logical extension of this argument should preclude lineups that include members similar only with respect to these features. Thus, especially in cross-racial identifications, lineup participants should be similar to each other in ways that extend beyond what could be termed "race cumulative" attributes.

Finally, in terms of lineup composition in instances with multiple suspects, officers should only place one suspect on the lineup at a time.[373] The more suspects there are in the lineup, the less the lineup serves as a test, and the higher the dangerous error rate—as more mistakes will be perceived as "confirmation" of an innocent suspect's guilt. That is, while a lineup's general error rate may be 35 percent (with five fillers and one suspect yielding an approximately 6-percent dangerous error rate), three different suspects and three fillers will yield about a 17.5-percent dangerous error rate.[374] This last practice—of placing more than one suspect in a given six-person lineup—frequently occurs in some police departments.[375]

---

[369] Farmer, John.

[370] California Penal Code § 859.7(a)(5) (2018).

[371] Natarajan, Radha. 1841.

[372] Ibid.

[373] Wells, Gary L. "Eyewitness Identification: Systemic Reforms." 641.

[374] Technically, if police officers are particularly eager to let a witness view two or more suspects in one lineup, they should—at the very least—have five fillers *per suspect* instead of merely having a total of five fillers plus the various suspects.

[375] Wells, Gary L. "Eyewitness Identification: Systemic Reforms." 641.

These composition changes should help ensure that lineups test witness memory as they should. However, the implementation of some of these recommendations may be subjective. For example, ensuring that the suspect does not "stand out" can be interpreted in many ways, with varying degrees of vigilance. Therefore, all lineup administrators should preserve photo records of the lineups. Currently, the photos from photo lineups are provided to defense counsel in most jurisdictions.[376] However, the same does not apply to live lineups. In order to equip defense counsel to identify irregularities in the lineups, the participants in live lineups should be photographed—on the day of the lineup—for defense counsel to examine and possibly use as evidence at trial.

This leads to the following policy recommendations:

REFORM #5: Lineup Composition Changes

> **5A:** Lineups should always have five or more filler individuals.

> **5B:** Only one suspect should be included in each lineup.

> **5C:** The suspect's facial and other features should not stand out in the lineup. Lineup participants should be similar to each other in ways that extend beyond what could be termed "race cumulative" attributes.

> **5D:** Defense counsel should be provided with a visual record of the lineup.

> > **I.** In photo lineups, defense counsel should be provided with the photos that were used.

> > **II.** In live lineups, defense counsel should be provided with photographs of the lineup

---

[376] Personal Communication with Gary Koepell, Deputy District Attorney for Contra Costa County, California.

members, and these photos should be taken on the day of the live lineup.

Reform #6: Immediate Measures of Witness Confidence and Observation Details

As discussed in previous chapters, courts and juries use witness confidence to determine the reliability of an identification. Confidence plays a role in the admissibility and believability of eyewitness testimony, despite its current negligible relationship with accuracy. However, the primary reason for confidence's current independence from accuracy relates to the overpowering effects of positive feedback to the witness.[377] Whatever small relationship may exist between accuracy and confidence is destroyed with the lineup administrator's confirmation—verbal, nonverbal, and often unintentional—discussion with a fellow witness, and especially the eventual sight of the identified suspect at trial.[378] The same applies to the witness's retrospective report of the details surrounding the observation, including the lighting, the duration of the event, how close the witness was, and other facts that may have a bearing on the accuracy of the identification.[379]

Various state commissions, including commissions in Illinois and North Carolina, have recommended a recording of witness confidence at the time of the identification.[380] New Jersey requires its jurisdictions to record witness confidence.[381] As does California.[382] However, few of these recommendations include requirements for

---

[377] TerBeek, Calvin. 26 (citing Wells, Gary L. and Eric P. Seelau. "Eyewitness Identification: Psychological Research and Legal Policy on Lineups." Psychology, Public Policy and Law, 1995, 1).
[378] TerBeek, Calvin. 26.
[379] TerBeek, Calvin. 26 (citing Wells, Gary L. and Eric P. Seelau. 1).
[380] Collins, Winn S. 11; Ehlers, Scott. "Eyewitness Identification: State Law Reform." *Champion*, National Association of Criminal Defense Lawyers, April 2005, 34.
[381] Farmer, John.
[382] California Penal Code § 859.7(a)(11) (2018).

recording the details surrounding the observation, which—according
to eyewitness expert and psychology professor Gary Wells—is as
much affected by positive feedback as confidence.[383] Furthermore,
other commission reports and reform recommendations overlook any
method of collecting the witness's perspective at the time of the
identification (including the previously noted Boston 2004 task force
recommendations heralded as the eyewitness identification "gold
standard").[384] This helps explain why few police agencies are
employing this relatively simple step, which not only helps juries but
also provides better indications of reliability to courts operating under
the *Biggers* standard for admissibility.[385]

Moreover, this recommendation can be fully effective only
when applied in conjunction with recommendation number two, that
lineup administrators be unaware of the actual suspect. If this is not the
case, then the recording of confidence and details may just as well be
affected by the unintentional nonverbal behavior of the administrator,
which may either influence or confirm a witness's choice.[386]

What's more, lineup administrators should also record the
length of time it takes the witness to make the identification. This is
yet another measure that no current reform proposal or
misidentification article recommends, despite the fact that previous
studies I have discussed mention this as one indicator of witness
accuracy. Like all identification details, a witness's retrospective
report of response time is likely to vary based on the post-
identification feedback. As no reform proposals even suggest that
response time be recorded, it logically follows that no reforms suggest
the testing of this at the time of identification (before the witness
receives confirmatory feedback). As police agencies following these
recommendations will already be recording confidence and
observation details at the identification anyway, I believe the benefit to

---

[383] TerBeek, Calvin. 26.
[384] "Task Force Recommendations on Eyewitness Identification." 16.
[385] Wells, Gary L. "Eyewitness Identification: Systemic Reforms." 642.
[386] TerBeek, Calvin. 26 (citing Wells, Gary L. and Eric P. Seelau. 1).

measuring response time vastly outweighs any inconvenience it might cause.

Finally, in implementing this last reform of measuring response time, we still cannot forget how cross-racial identifications need to be treated differently in many instances—eyewitness response time is just one example of the need for this different treatment. As previously discussed studies show, response time does not correlate with accuracy for cross-racial identifications.[387] Therefore, while this should be measured in all instances (as the existence of mixed-race individuals means that lineup administrators may not be best equipped to immediately know the race of the suspect and eyewitness), in cases where cross-racial identification has occurred, the response time should not be considered by judges or revealed to the jury, as it would be misleading.

This leads to the following policy recommendations:

REFORM #6: Immediate Measures of Witness Confidence and Observation Details

    6A: Immediately after a witness makes an identification, the witness should be asked to describe his or her level of confidence. This should be recorded by the lineup administrator.[388]

    6B: Immediately after a witness makes an identification— or any time before this point—the witness should be asked a number of questions designed to solicit the details surrounding the witness's observation of the culprit. These comments should be recorded.

---

[387] Natarajan, Radha. 1838–1839.

[388] Crucially, some of the benefits of the double-blind administration are lost if the confidence statement is made to a "non-blind" officer (i.e., an officer who knows whether the identification was made of the suspect).

6C: Lineup administrators should record the approximate time it takes the witness to identify the suspect (the timing should start when the witness is presented with the suspect's photo in a sequential lineup). When a cross-racial identification has occurred, the court should not consider this factor in determining reliability, and the jury should not be provided with this information.

Additionally, I believe that this reform is most effective when employed in conjunction with the next two reforms: statutory allowance of expert testimony and misidentification jury instructions. This is because experts and evidence-based jury instructions can provide jurors with the information that is necessary to properly interpret the results of these measures. For example, at-identification confidence level correlates with accuracy while at-trial confidence level does not.

Chapter 4.4: Explanation of Tier-Two Reforms (Seven and Eight)

The following two reforms are the second aspect of my two-tiered approach to reducing faulty convictions based on misidentification. The previous recommendations are all intended to reduce misidentifications (with the exception of reform six, which requires the seventh and eighth reforms to be fully effective). That is, the previous reforms are part of "tier one" because they work to reduce faulty convictions by reducing the ultimate source: the misidentifications themselves.

"Tier two," as I conceive of it, works to reduce faulty convictions by increasing the post-identification protections that jurors have against being mistakenly deceived. Tier two, in short, assumes that the tier one reforms cannot be perfectly effective. Some scholarly publications mention the problems of insufficient experts or jury instructions. Fewer publications suggest that changes in these areas can help. The only in-depth suggestion for expert and instruction-related reforms was in Ms. Natarajan's cross-racial identification article, and they solely regarded cross-racial issues. And no major government commission or national organization that I have encountered made any comprehensive reform suggestions that encompassed what I would call this tier-two issue.

In the face of this trend for police procedure-oriented misidentification reform, I believe that equipping jurors to identify misidentifications is a necessary aspect in the effort to decrease faulty convictions in this area.

Reform #7: General Statutory Allowance of Misidentification Experts at Trial

Ignorance on the part of the jury is yet another factor facilitating faulty convictions based on misidentifications, and expert witnesses are often barred from countering this ignorance. As I concluded in the chapter on case law, a lack of jurisprudential guidance (that is, clearly put and consistent case law) on this matter has let judges use their own discretion, often leading to the exclusion of this expert testimony (i.e., the experts are not allowed to testify).[389] Yet, despite the precedent and "common sense" leading judges to believe that "juries are well aware of the problems inherent in eyewitness identifications," jurors frequently rely on false identifications and inaccurate post-identification cues, accepting eyewitness testimony as "absolute proof."[390] Thus, state law must explicitly allow expert testimony on this matter.

Traditionally, the testimony of expert witnesses is used to help jurors understand issues that are beyond what a lay person could be expected to know. Rule 702 of the Federal Rules of Evidence, which most states use as a model, notes that experts may testify as to their conclusions "[i]f scientific, technical, or other specialized knowledge will assist the [juror]" in understanding an item of evidence, assuming

---

[389] Natarajan, Radha. 1833.
[390] Clements, Noah. 284; Gambell, Suzannah. 191.

the given expert witness is qualified in the area of specialized knowledge about which they are concluding and, generally speaking, bases his or her conclusions on applicable and "reliable principles and methods."[391] For example, a medical doctor may help a jury understand the nature of a knife wound so that the jury can better determine whether a defendant is guilty of attempted murder.

As the field of psychology is considered a science, psychologists are frequently able to testify when judges determine that they will be able to assist the jury in coming to a conclusion. Most misidentification experts are technically psychologists, and, as the dangers—and intricacies—of eyewitness misidentification are becoming better known, some courts are "allowing psychologists to testify about problems associated with eyewitness identification."[392] A substantial portion of courts, however, still prohibit testimony on misidentification, mostly for the reasons discussed in the case law.[393] Thus, the slow trend towards admitting expert testimony is useless for a large number of defendants.

As I mentioned earlier, my overarching recommendation will be for the passage of state law that establishes these eight reforms. However, for this and the next reform, the significance of a clear state law takes on greater meaning. Of the literature I encountered, the few articles that mention a potential for changing expert testimony standards seem to lament the current state of expert admissibility as though only the Supreme Court—or courts in general—can change the frequency with which misidentification experts are allowed to testify. However, unclear and seemingly organic case law need not be the only foundation on which experts are admitted. Case law often interprets statutes.[394] Thus, an explicit statute on the admissibility of eyewitness

---

[391] Rule 702. Federal Rules of Evidence, Article VII, http://www.law.cornell.edu/rules/fre/rules.htm#Rule702, accessed on April 7, 2008.
[392] Tanford, J.A. "Law Reform by Courts, Legislatures, and Commissions Following Empirical Research on Jury Instructions." *Law and Society Review*, vol. 25, no. 1, 1990, 155.
[393] Natarajan, Radha. 1833.
[394] Ibid.

identification experts could potentially settle the issue for each state. Granted, the fifty states have various standards in place for expert witnesses, and it would be a complicated issue to sort through the different statutory requirements for each state. Nonetheless, a direct approach to this issue (i.e., a state law explicitly allowing this type of testimony) would solve the problem of unclear case law, settle the dispute over the admissibility of expert witnesses, and—most importantly—give jurors the assistance they need in evaluating a great deal of psychological information.

Indeed, the vast amount of data on the subject is yet another reason why experts are so important—and why jury instructions can never be as effective as a live expert testifying in court. The more information states pack into jury instructions on misidentification, the harder it will be for jurors to synthesize the material. Experts are in a better position to explain the dangers of misidentification, the cues for accuracy, and how these factors apply to the case at hand. Furthermore, this is especially the case with the counter-intuitive facts that jurors may find difficult to believe from a written jury instruction, including, for example, the fact that racial attitudes play no role in cross-racial misidentification rates and the fact that confidence at the time of the trial is completely unrelated to accuracy.

Finally, yet another issue related to experts is the scope with which they are allowed to testify.[395] The Assistant Public Defender for the State of New Jersey, Joseph Krakora, noted that "experts are never permitted... to offer an opinion that a particular ID is in fact mistaken or likely to be so."[396] Throughout other jurisdictions and in other states, the scope of expert testimony ranges widely.[397] While it does not seem appropriate for an expert to declare that an identification was inaccurate, confining experts to general terms may not allow them to speak to the specifics of the case. For example, a court's understanding

---

[395] Personal communications with Joseph Krakora, Assistant Public Defender for New Jersey. April 6, 2008.
[396] Ibid.
[397] Ibid.

that expert testimony is limited to the generalities of misidentification could lead the judge to prevent a discussion of the dangers of cross-racial identifications.

In short, the preponderance of the psychological evidence on the subject indicates that jurors need help evaluating eyewitnesses. They need help understanding the general fallibility and the cues for determining the accuracy of eyewitness identifications. They need help that is tailored to the specifics of the case at hand. State law should explicitly recognize the field of psychology as it relates to eyewitness identifications, establish the relevance of this testimony, and permit a discussion that addresses the specific misidentification issues of concern.

This leads to the following policy recommendation:

REFORM #7: General Statutory Allowance of Misidentification Experts at Trial

7A: State law should explicitly allow the testimony of eyewitness misidentification experts in all eyewitness identification cases (as even identifications resulting from perfect police procedure are subject to the same weaknesses of human memory).

7B: The scope of expert testimony must be wide enough to cover the specifics of the case at hand, assuming the expert can still present findings that are based on reliable principles established in his or her field. This is particularly the case for trials with cross-racial identifications.

Reform #8: Jury Instructions on Misidentification and Accuracy Cues

Eyewitness identification experts are not the only way for juries to learn about eyewitness misidentification. Jurors need to know the general dangers and proper accuracy cues related to eyewitness testimony. A way to guarantee at least some basic level of knowledge is through jury instructions.

In all U.S. states, the jury instruction phase involves the judge directing the jury as to how they should deliberate and often what types of factors to consider. The instructions are usually based on the law. For example, a judge might explain how the jury must find a defendant innocent unless they are convinced of guilt "beyond a reasonable doubt." Most states currently have instructions that already relate to witness testimony and witness reliability. For example, the California Criminal Jury Instructions reads:

> In evaluating a witness's testimony, you may consider anything that reasonably tests to prove or disprove the truth or accuracy of that testimony. Among the factors that you may consider are:
>
> - How well could the witness see, hear, or otherwise perceive the things about which the witness testified?
>
> - How well was the witness able to remember and describe what happened?[398]

This California list itemizes twelve more factors. While the two example factors above are questions, some of the instructions are direct suggestions, including one suggestion to disregard a witness's testimony if he or she lied about an important fact.[399] These specifically listed factors, like most jury instructions, are based on a combination of statutes and case law, established by the legislature and courts, respectively.[400] Significantly, however, all case-law-based instructions are developed through a court's attempt to interpret the

---

[398] California Criminal Jury Instructions. Section 105: Witnesses, Judicial Council of California, 2005, http://www2.courtinfo.ca.gov/crimjuryinst/, accessed on April 4, 2008.
[399] Ibid.
[400] Ibid.

law. Therefore, assuming that a law providing for jury instructions does not contradict another state law or criminal code, there need not be any worry that legislatively created jury instructions would be overruled by existing case law based on state law. And, while some of the limited jury instructions on misidentification are based on Supreme Court rulings—simply listing the *Biggers* factors—these may, in fact, be the most in need of correction (as *Biggers*, more often than not, leads jurors in the wrong direction).

While jury instructions on witness reliability are often noncommittal and delivered in the form of questions—as the example above illustrates—instructions on this issue would need to be specific and clearly state which post-identification cues correlate with accuracy. The importance of this is particularly clear if we recall how the vague cross-racial identification instructions (asking the jury to simply consider whether the identification was cross-racial) were capable of *mis*informing juries, leading them to believe that cross-racial identifications were more reliable than same-race identifications.[401]

Jury instructions are perhaps the most important part of this second-tier approach to limiting faulty convictions based on misidentifications. Of all the articles, books, commission recommendations, and government guidelines that I viewed, virtually none consider this two-tier approach. And of those articles that address jury instructions tangentially or in a limited capacity, none places the instructions (or expert testimony) nearly on par with the other reform ideas. Given the psychological potential for misidentification—even with non-suggestive procedure—this single-minded pursuit of police procedure reform fails to fully protect innocent suspects. When jurors are informed of the misidentification dangers, they will be less likely to blindly believe that eyewitnesses are presenting "absolute proof."[402] And when jurors learn how different post-identification cues correspond with accuracy while other "common sense" factors do not,

---

[401] Natarajan, Radha. 1842.
[402] Clements, Noah. 284; Gambell, Suzannah. 191.

they will be better able to discriminate between accurate and inaccurate identifications, increasing reliance on the former as much as decreasing reliance on the latter.

This leads to the following policy recommendations:

REFORM #8: Jury Instructions

> **8A:** Jury instructions should be created to clearly warn jurors of the dangers of misidentification and the high rate of misidentification as observed in psychological studies.

> **8B:** Jury instructions should mention the known dangers of cross-racial identification.

>> **I.** The instructions should mention that cross-racial identifications have a higher likelihood of error, regardless of the racial attitudes of the witness.

>> **II.** The instructions should mention that, while the prior description of a culprit may indicate reliability, it does not indicate reliability when the description was "race cumulative."

>> **III.** If recommendation 6C is not followed, and a witness or investigator mentions a witness's response time in identifying a suspect, a jury instruction should be read establishing that there is no relation between response time and accuracy in cross-racial identifications.

> **8C:** Jury instructions should mention the post-identification cues that psychological evidence has identified.

>> **I.** The instructions should include the cues that are associated with accuracy.

II. The instructions should provide warnings regarding the commonly used cues that do not necessarily correlate with accuracy (especially the cue of confidence in identifications that did not have double-blind administration and immediate recording of confidence at the time of identification).

Chapter 4.5: Final Recommendation and Conclusion

These eight general reforms are necessary to significantly reduce the likelihood of faulty convictions based on eyewitness misidentification. The two-tier approach I have put forth presents the best chance of protecting innocent suspects by reducing the false identifications while also combating the ignorance that supports them. Yet, even though some of these reform ideas have existed for years (namely, the non-race and non-lap-related aspects of reforms one, two, three, and five), not enough jurisdictions employ them as the default procedures.[403] Despite the existence of these reform ideas, misidentification reform is clearly moving at a dangerously slow pace.

Misidentification expert Gary Well's 2006 reform analysis identifies poor communication, police tradition, a lack of incentives, and local control as the primary impediments to reform.[404] Essentially, most people do not know about the existent psychological data, police departments base current practices on past practices, neither prosecutors nor courts force police to change their procedures, and "[the] 13,000 law enforcement departments" are left pretty much alone.[405] While all these factors probably contribute to maintaining the *status quo*, I find the last factor—local autonomy—to be the most compelling. Police procedure and courtroom practices are not changing as they should because each local police agency is free to set

---

[403] Clements, Noah. 287.
[404] Wells, Gary L. "Eyewitness Identification: Systemic Reforms." 632–635.
[405] Ibid. 633.

its own procedure as it sees fit, while local courts are free to do the same based on the lack of clarity in case law. And my analysis of several major forces for reform confirms that this factor overshadows all others in stagnating reform.

The states that seem to have taken eyewitness identification reform seriously have nearly all created state commissions that, in turn, urge local law enforcement agencies to change their practices.[406] Obviously, "urging" is not enough. By and large, these agencies have been slow to respond, if they respond at all.[407] For example, the Illinois Commission on Capital Punishment recommended a number of eyewitness identification reforms in 2002. Since then, three reforms were implemented in a never-ending pilot program (these reforms were effectively 1A, 2A, and 3A from my lists above). The only reform that all police agencies adopted was the instruction regarding the possible absence of the suspect (reform 3, above), and this has only occurred because of a 2003 state law that the legislature passed.[408] Commissions in North Carolina, Wisconsin, and Virginia were similarly toothless, merely recommending that police departments adopt certain practices without forcing action.[409] The U.S. Department of Justice's 1999 recommendations on lineup construction and witness instructions were similarly optional, as the federal government has no jurisdiction.[410] Even authors and scholars lamenting the state of confusing or scientifically incorrect case law urge individual courts to reject precedent or, in a recipe for potentially slower reform, simply appeal to "the United States Supreme court to step in and mandate a new standard for eyewitness review" in some type of *deus ex machina* approach.[411] It appears that general recommendations, local control,

---

[406] Ehlers, Scott. 34; Kolbuchar, Amy, et al. 387.
[407] Wells, Gary L. "Eyewitness Identification: Systemic Reforms." 635.
[408] Ehlers, Scott. 43.
[409] Ehlers, Scott. 34; Kolbuchar, Amy, et al. 387; TerBeek, Calvin. 47; Wells, Gary L. "Eyewitness Identification: Systemic Reforms." 641.
[410] Kolbuchar, Amy, et al. 387.
[411] TerBeek, Calvin. 48.

and reliance on local initiative will only continue the slow pace at which police agencies are adopting reforms.

It is for these reasons that I believe state legislation mandating specific police and court practice presents the best chance of ensuring that these reforms actually occur. While individual police agency autonomy has its benefits, only unequivocal new standards can overcome the stagnant, piecemeal approach that has characterized eyewitness identification reform for the past three decades.

While the specific means of achieving this aim would fill another book, one place to start may be the American Law Institute (ALI), which creates "model codes" and suggested statutes for lawmaking bodies to adopt.[412] If these reforms, or some variation thereof, were passed though the ALI's multi-stage, multi-draft process and suggested as the model state law in the area of eyewitness identification procedure, reformers would be somewhat more equipped to advocate for this significant and comprehensive legislation.

Changing state law in all fifty states will be an enormous task. However, given the dangers of eyewitness misidentification, it is necessary. Human psychology, police procedure, juror ignorance, and unhelpful case law together cause more faulty convictions than all other sources combined. Only with this two-tiered, race-conscious approach to the problem can the criminal justice system balance the interests of law enforcement with the dire need to protect innocent suspects. Thus, these eight reforms present our best hope in the effort to eliminate the pervasive and institutionalized threat of witness misidentification.

---

[412] "About the American Law Institute." Brochure, American Law Institute, http://www.ali.org/doc/thisIsALI.pdf, accessed on April 5, 2008.

Appendix A

Frequency of Written Policies Regarding Eyewitness Identifications

One of the primary difficulties in reforming eyewitness identification procedures is that most law enforcement agencies do not even have written policies in place.

In 2014, the U.S. Department of Justice issued a grant to the Police Executive Research Forum (PERF) in order to conduct a national survey of eyewitness identification procedures. The PERF, a non-profit police research and policy organization, surveyed hundreds of law enforcement agencies of various sizes.

The PERF published its findings in 2014 in a U.S. Department of Justice research report titled "A National Survey of Eyewitness Identification Procedures in Law Enforcement Agencies." Among the PERF's findings was the discovery that most agencies do not even have written procedures in place for how sworn officers conduct identifications with witnesses. Table 8 of the report is reproduced on the following page, with content bolded for emphasis. While large agencies (those with over 500 sworn officers) are more likely to have policies in place, the percentage with no policy in place is still quite high.

Procedure	Existence of Policy	Size of Agency (No. of Sworn Officers)					Total
		≤ 25	26–50	51–99	100–499	≥ 500	All agencies
Show-Ups n=580	No Policy	82.20%	74.50%	66.00%	58.50%	33.30%	77.10%
	Policy for Construction OR Administration	3.00%	1.90%	4.30%	7.30%	11.10%	3.30%
	Policy for Construction & Administration	14.90%	23.60%	29.80%	34.10%	55.60%	19.70%
Photo Lineups n=584	No Policy	72.00%	61.70%	47.90%	28.60%	25.00%	64.40%
	Policy for Construction OR Administration	6.60%	6.60%	6.30%	7.20%	12.50%	6.70%
	Policy for Construction & Administration	21.40%	31.80%	45.80%	64.30%	62.50%	28.90%
Live Lineups n=595	No Policy	84.10%	89.70%	79.20%	82.90%	50.00%	84.20%
	Policy for Construction OR Administration	1.50%	0.90%	2.10%	0%	0%	1.30%
	Policy for Construction & Administration	14.30%	9.30%	18.80%	17.10%	50.00%	14.50%
Composites n=592	No Policy	91.00%	94.30%	85.10%	90.50%	71.40%	90.90%
	Policy for Construction OR Administration	1.50%	0.00%	2.10%	2.40%	0.00%	1.40%
	Policy for Construction & Administration	7.40%	5.70%	12.80%	7.10%	28.60%	7.80%
Mugshot Searches n=595	No Policy	92.60%	92.50%	87.80%	92.70%	87.50%	92.10%
	Policy for Construction OR Administration	2.30%	0.90%	2.00%	2.40%	0.00%	2.00%
	Policy for Construction & Administration	5.10%	6.60%	10.20%	4.90%	12.50%	5.90%

Source: A National Survey of Eyewitness Identification Procedures in Law Enforcement Agencies, Research Report Submitted to US Department of Justice, June 1, 2014. Police Executive Research Forum.

Appendix B

A Model State Law Addressing Witness Misidentification: West Virginia's Eyewitness Identification Act

The state of West Virginia has a set of state laws that serve as a national model for reforming eyewitness identification procedures. These laws address sequential lineups, blind administration, law enforcement training, standard procedures for state and local agencies, and clear rules regarding witness instructions and lineup construction.

West Virginia's eyewitness reform procedures are outlined in the West Virginia Code, Chapter 62, Article 1E.

WEST VIRGINIA CODE
CHAPTER 62—CRIMINAL PROCEDURE
ARTICLE 1E. EYEWITNESS IDENTIFICATION ACT.

§62-1E-1. Definitions.

For the purposes of this article:

(1) "Administrator" means the person conducting the live lineup, photo lineup, or showup.

(2) "Suspect" means the person believed by law enforcement to be the possible perpetrator of the crime.

(3) "Blind" means the administrator does not know the identity of the suspect.

(4) "Blinded" means the administrator may know who the suspect is but does not know which lineup member is being viewed by the eyewitness.

(5) "Eyewitness" means a person whose identification of another person may be relevant in a criminal proceeding.

(6) "Filler" means either a person or a photograph of a person who is not suspected of an offense and is included in an identification procedure.

(7) "Folder shuffle method" means a procedure for displaying a photo lineup with the following steps:

(A) Photos used in a photo lineup are placed in their own respective folder, and the folders are shuffled, numbered, and then presented to an eyewitness such that the administrator cannot see or track which photo is being presented to the witness until after the procedure is completed;

(B) The procedure is completed only when the eyewitness has viewed the entire array of numbered folders, even if an affirmative identification is made prior to the eyewitness viewing all of the numbered folders;

(C) If an eyewitness requests a second viewing, the eyewitness must be shown all of the lineup members again, even if the eyewitness makes an identification during this second showing; and

(D) The eyewitness shall be allowed to review the folders only once after the initial viewing is complete.

(8) "Lineup" means a live lineup or photo lineup of persons or photographs of persons matching as close as possible the eyewitness's description of the perpetrator.

(9) "Live lineup" means a procedure in which a group of people is displayed to an eyewitness for the purpose of determining if the eyewitness is able to identify the perpetrator of a crime.

(10) "Photo lineup" means a procedure in which an array of photographs is displayed to an eyewitness for the purpose of determining if the eyewitness is able to identify the perpetrator of a crime.

(11) "Sequential presentation" means presenting live or photo lineup persons to the eyewitness one-by-one rather than all at once.

(12) "Showup" means an identification procedure in which an eyewitness is presented with a single suspect for the purpose of determining whether the eyewitness identifies this individual as the perpetrator.

§62-1E-2. Eyewitness identification procedures.

110

(a) Prior to a lineup or showup, law enforcement should record as complete a description as possible of the perpetrator provided by the eyewitness, in the eyewitness's own words. This statement should also include information regarding the conditions under which the eyewitness observed the perpetrator including location, time, distance, obstructions, lighting and weather conditions. The eyewitness should also be asked if he or she wears or has been prescribed glasses or contact lenses and whether he or she was wearing them at the time of the witnessed event. The administrator should record whether or not the eyewitness was wearing glasses or contact lenses at the time of the lineup or showup.

(b) After completing the requirements of subsection (a) of this section, but before a lineup or showup, the eyewitness should be given the following instructions:

(1) That the perpetrator may or may not be present in the lineup, or, in the case of a showup, may or may not be the person that is presented to the eyewitness;

(2) That the eyewitness is not required to make an identification;

(3) That it is as important to exclude innocent persons as it is to identify the perpetrator;

(4) That the investigation will continue whether or not an identification is made; and

(5) That the administrator does not know the identity of the perpetrator.

(c) Nothing should be said, shown, or otherwise suggested to the eyewitness that might influence the eyewitness's identification of any particular lineup or showup member, at any time prior to, during, or following a lineup or showup.

(d) All lineups should be conducted blind unless to do so would place an undue burden on law enforcement or the investigation. If conducting a blind lineup would place an undue burden on law enforcement or the investigation, then the administrator shall use the folder shuffle method.

(e) All lineups should be conducted in a sequential presentation. When there are multiple suspects, each identification procedure shall include only one suspect.

(f) At least four fillers should be used in all lineups. The fillers shall resemble the description of the suspect as much as practicable and shall not unduly stand out.

(g) In a photo lineup, there should be no characteristics of the photos themselves or the background context in which they are placed which shall make any of the photos unduly stand out.

(h) In a live lineup, all lineup participants must be out of view of the eyewitness prior to the identification procedure.

(i) If there are multiple eyewitnesses for the same lineup:

(1) Each eyewitness should view the lineup or lineups separately;

(2) The suspect should be placed in a different position in the lineup for each eyewitness; and

(3) The eyewitnesses should not be permitted to communicate with each other until all identification procedures have been completed.

(j) Showups should only be performed using a live suspect and only in exigent circumstances that require the immediate display of a suspect to an eyewitness. A law-enforcement official shall not conduct a showup with a single photo; rather a photo lineup must be used.

(k) Law-enforcement officers should make a written or video record of a lineup which shall be provided to the prosecuting attorney in the event that any person is charged with the offense under investigation. The written record shall include all steps taken to comply with this article which shall include the following information:

(1) The date, time, and location of the lineup;

(2) The names of every person in the lineup, if known, and all other persons present at the lineup;

(3) The words used by the eyewitness in any identification, including words that describe the eyewitness's certainty or uncertainty in the identification at the time the identification is made;

(4) Whether it was a photo lineup or live lineup;

(5) The number of photos or individuals that were presented in the lineup;

(6) Whether the lineup administrator knew which person in the lineup was the suspect;

(7) Whether, before the lineup, the eyewitness was instructed that the perpetrator might or might not be presented in the lineup;

(8) Whether the lineup was simultaneous or sequential;

(9) The signature, or initials, of the eyewitness, or notation if the eyewitness declines or is unable to sign; and

(10) A video of the lineup and the eyewitness's response may be included.

§62-1E-3. Training of law-enforcement officers.

The Superintendent of State Police may create educational materials and conduct training programs to instruct law-enforcement officers and recruits how to conduct lineups in compliance with this section. Any West Virginia law-enforcement agency, as defined in section one, article twenty-nine, chapter thirty of this code, conducting eyewitness identification procedures shall adopt specific written procedures for conducting photo lineups, live lineups, and showups that comply with this article on or before January 1, 2014.

Appendix C

States' Efforts to Address Witness Misidentification

Various states have taken steps to combat the problem of witness misidentification. While not every state has followed all the available best practices, substantial progress has already been made on a variety of fronts, which are outlined below:

Procedure	States implementing procedure
Blind administration of line-ups	Connecticut, North Carolina, Ohio, Texas, West Virginia, Vermont, Wisconsin
Law enforcement training	North Carolina, West Virginia
Lineup construction guidelines	Illinois, Ohio, Vermont, West Virginia
Clear witness instructions	Illinois, North Carolina, Ohio, West Virginia
Sequential line-up procedure	Connecticut, North Carolina, West Virginia, Wisconsin

Appendix D

Partial List of Innocent People Wrongfully Convicted Due to Witness Misidentification

Witness misidentification destroys the lives of innocent people. This fact must always be kept in mind while discussing statistics and abstract policy reforms.

The National Registry of Exonerations (NRE) keeps track of individuals who were proven innocent or otherwise exonerated after having been convicted. The NRE is a joint project of the University of California, Irvine; the University of Michigan Law School, and Michigan State University School of Law.

The following list provides the names, sentences, and other key information for people who were wrongfully convicted when at least one factor in the conviction was witness misidentification. It is not a list of all the innocent people wrongfully convicted through misidentification. It is only a list of those innocent people whose innocence has been proven by DNA or other incontrovertible evidence. Thus, it is only a partial list of the people who are suffering or who have suffered as a result of witness misidentification.

States and localities must implement the policies outlined in this book if we are to stop this list from getting longer.

Last Name	First Name	State	Crime	Sentence	Convicted	Exonerated
Abbitt	Joseph Lamont	NC	Child Sex Abuse	Life	1995	2009
Abdal	Warith Habib	NY	Sexual Assault	20 to Life	1983	1999
Abney	Quentin	NY	Robbery	20 to Life	2006	2012
Adams	Kenneth	IL	Murder	75 years	1978	1996
Adams	Randall Dale	TX	Murder	Death	1977	1989
Alejandro	Gilbert	TX	Sexual Assault	12 years	1990	1994
Alexander	Malcolm	LA	Sexual Assault	Life without parole	1980	2018
Alexander	Richard	IN	Sexual Assault	70 years	1998	2001
Allen	Christopher	IN	Murder	144 years	2002	2006

Last Name	First Name	State	Crime	Sentence	Convicted	Exonerated
Allen	Dante	OH	Kidnapping	Not sentenced	2005	2005
Allen	Dennis	TX	Murder	Life	2000	2019
Alonzo	Quintin	TX	Murder	Life	2003	2019
Alvarez	Roy	CA	Robbery	14 years	1995	2002
Amezquita	Gilbert	TX	Assault	15 years	1998	2007
Anderson	Eric	MI	Robbery	15 to 22 years	2010	2019
Anderson	James C.	NY	Burglary/Unlawful Entry	Not sentenced	1990	1990
Anderson	Marvin	VA	Sexual Assault	Life	1982	2002
Anderson	Roland	MS	Assault	15 years	1997	2007
Appling	Riolordo	CA	Assault	Not sentenced	2012	2013
Arrington	Jermaine	MD	Murder	25 years	1995	2010
Arroyo	Rogelio	IL	Murder	Life without parole	1982	1991
Arteaga	Jose	CA	Theft	116 days	2016	2016
Atkins	Herman	CA	Sexual Assault	47 years	1988	2000
Atkins	Timothy	CA	Murder	32 to Life	1987	2007
Atlas	Gerald	CA	Attempted Murder	28 to life	1990	1998
August	Adrienne	TX	Burglary/Unlawful Entry	20 years	2018	2019
Avery	Chamar	MI	Murder	20 to 50 years	2000	2010
Avery	Steven	WI	Attempted Murder	32 years	1985	2003
Aviles	Anselmo	MA	Sexual Assault	16 to 18 years	1989	1997
Ayers	Randall Lynn	OH	Attempted Murder	14 to 50 years	1982	1990
Bain	James	FL	Child Sex Abuse	Life	1974	2009
Baker	Dontrell	FL	Robbery	Not sentenced	1997	1997
Bankhead	Antoine	MO	Murder	Life	2002	2006
Barbour	Bennett	VA	Sexual Assault	10 years	1978	2012
Barner	Glenn	CA	Robbery	16 years	1992	1993
Barnes	Steven	NY	Murder	25 to Life	1989	2009
Barnhouse	William	IN	Sexual Assault	80 years	1992	2017
Batten	Floyd	NY	Murder	20 to life	1984	2004
Bauer	Chester	MT	Sexual Assault	30 years	1983	1997
Beaver	Antonio	MO	Robbery	18 years	1997	2007
Beckett	Dale	OH	Murder	15 to Life	1997	2003
Bell	Derrick	NY	Robbery	12 1/2 to 25 years	1997	2007

116

Last Name	First Name	State	Crime	Sentence	Convicted	Exonerated
Bellamy	Kareem	NY	Murder	25 to Life	1995	2011
Benitez	Ricardo	NY	Robbery	22 to life	2010	2015
Beranek	Richard	WI	Sexual Assault	243 years	1990	2018
Berry	DeMarlo	NV	Murder	Life	1995	2017
Berry	Johnny	PA	Murder	Life without parole	1995	2019
Berryman	Earl	NJ	Sexual Assault	50 years	1985	1997
Bibbins	Gene	LA	Child Sex Abuse	Life	1987	2003
Blackmon	Eric	IL	Murder	60 years	2004	2019
Blair	Michael	TX	Murder	Death	1994	2008
Blake	Bryan	NY	Murder	25 to life	1985	1989
Bloodsworth	Kirk	MD	Murder	Death	1985	1993
Blyden	Malisha	NY	Attempted Murder	40 years	2007	2014
Bolden	Eddie	IL	Murder	Life without parole	1996	2016
Bolduc	Frank	F-WI	Robbery	48 years and 4 months	1991	1999
Bolstad	Daniel	WI	Sexual Assault	20 years	2007	2015
Booker	Donte	OH	Sexual Assault	10 to 25 years	1987	2005
Boone	Otis	NY	Robbery	25 years	2012	2019
Booth	Darrell	CA	Murder	15 to Life	2011	2017
Boquete	Orlando	FL	Sexual Assault	65 years	1983	2006
Boyce	David	VA	Murder	Life	1991	2013
Boyette	Calvin	NY	Attempted Murder	12 1/2 to 25 years	1984	2001
Bradford	Ted	WA	Sexual Assault	10 years	1996	2010
Bragdon	Anthony	DC	Sexual Assault	30 years	1992	2003
Braunskill	Clarence	NY	Drug Possession or Sale	20 to 40 years	1990	1997
Bravo	Mark	CA	Sexual Assault	8 years	1990	1994
Bright	Dan L.	LA	Murder	Death	1996	2004
Brim	Dominique	MI	Assault	Not sentenced	2002	2002
Briscoe	Johnny	MO	Sexual Assault	45 years	1983	2006
Brison	Dale	PA	Sexual Assault	18 to 42 years	1991	1994
Brock	Donald	IL	Theft	Not sentenced	1989	1989
Bromgard	Jimmy Ray	MT	Child Sex Abuse	40 years	1987	2002
Brooks	Levon	MS	Murder	Life without parole	1992	2008
Brown	Alfred	TX	Murder	Death	2005	2015

117

Last Name	First Name	State	Crime	Sentence	Convicted	Exonerated
Brown	Danny	OH	Murder	Life	1982	2001
Brown	Dennis	LA	Sexual Assault	Life	1985	2005
Brown	Joyce Ann	TX	Murder	25 to Life	1980	1990
Brown	Nathan	LA	Sexual Assault	25 years	1997	2014
Brown	Patrick	PA	Robbery	22 to 70 years	2002	2010
Brown	Robert	IL	Murder	35 years	1984	1989
Brown	Tony	FL	Murder	Life	2010	2018
Brown, Jr.	Knolly	NC	Child Sex Abuse	5 to 6 3/4 years	2009	2016
Bryant	Andre	FL	Robbery	30 years	2007	2015
Bryant	Malcolm	MD	Murder	Life	1999	2016
Bryson	David	OK	Sexual Assault	85 years	1983	2003
Bullock	Ronnie	IL	Child Sex Abuse	60 years	1984	1994
Bunge	Charles	NY	Attempt, Violent	6 years	2007	2010
Bunkley	Derrick	MI	Attempted Murder	17 to 32 years	2014	2016
Bunn	John	NY	Murder	7 to life	1992	2018
Buntin	Harold	IN	Sexual Assault	50 years	1986	2007
Burnette	Victor	VA	Sexual Assault	20 years	1979	2009
Burnside	Brandon	WI	Murder	Life	2011	2015
Burt	Lazaro	NY	Murder	25 to Life	1994	2002
Bush	Gary	VA	Robbery	12 years	2007	2018
Butler, Jr.	A.B.	TX	Sexual Assault	Life	1983	2000
Byrd	Kevin	TX	Sexual Assault	Life	1985	1997
Cadogan	Donovan	WI	Other Nonviolent Felony	Life without parole	2013	2017
Cage	Dean	IL	Child Sex Abuse	40 years	1996	2008
Caldwell	Maurice	CA	Murder	27 to Life	1991	2011
Callace	Leonard	NY	Sexual Assault	25 to 50 years	1987	1992
Cameron	Darrell	IL	Robbery	Not sentenced	1991	1992
Campbell	Lori	GA	Theft	Probation	2005	2007
Campbell	Teshome	IL	Murder	55 years	1998	2016
Capozzi	Anthony	NY	Sexual Assault	11 to 35 years	1987	2007
Cardenas	Carlos	NY	Robbery	8 to 25 years	1996	2007
Cardenas	Napoleon	NY	Robbery	15 to 30 years	1999	2007
Carini	William	IL	Sexual Assault	26 years	1992	2017
Carmona	Arthur	CA	Robbery	12 years	1998	2000

118

Last Name	First Name	State	Crime	Sentence	Convicted	Exonerated
Carter	Edward	MI	Sexual Assault	Life	1975	2010
Carter	Steven	FL	Assault	Not sentenced	1990	1990
Cash	Tazell	MI	Robbery	10 to 20 years	2017	2019
Castillo	Sergio	TX	Attempted Murder	25 years	1994	2014
Cestoni	Enzo	F-CA	Weapon Possession or Sale	Not sentenced	2016	2016
Chalmers	Terry	NY	Sexual Assault	12 to 24 years	1987	1995
Chandler	Edwin	KY	Manslaughter	30 years	1995	2009
Chaparro	Anthony	NJ	Sexual Assault	Life	2003	2014
Chapman	Vernon	LA	Sexual Assault	Life	1980	1994
Charles	Clyde	LA	Sexual Assault	Life	1982	1999
Charles	Ulysses Rodriguez	MA	Sexual Assault	80 years	1984	2001
Chatman	Charles	TX	Sexual Assault	Life	1981	2008
Cheung	Kum Yet	CA	Attempt, Violent	29 years and 8 months	1995	2002
Childers	Brad	TX	Robbery	50 years	2004	2018
Clancy	Michael	NY	Murder	25 to Life	1999	2009
Clark	Robert	GA	Sexual Assault	Life	1982	2005
Clark, Jr.	Royal	LA	Robbery	49 years and six months	2003	2019
Clay	Frederick	MA	Murder	Life without parole	1981	2017
Clay, Sr.	David	MO	Murder	Life without parole	1988	1999
Clemmons	Eric	MO	Murder	Death	1987	2000
Clugston	Christopher	FL	Murder	Life	1983	2001
Coco	Allen	LA	Sexual Assault	Life	1997	2006
Cole	Timothy B.	TX	Sexual Assault	25 years	1986	2009
Coleman	Christopher	IL	Sexual Assault	60 years	1995	2014
Coney	Robert Carroll	TX	Robbery	Life	1966	2004
Connor	Matthew	PA	Murder	Life	1980	1990
Conteh	Maligie	VA	Robbery	1 year and 11 months	2010	2013
Contreras	Marco	CA	Attempted Murder	Life	1997	2017
Cooper	Keith	IN	Robbery	40 years	1997	2017
Cortez	George	PA	Murder	Life without parole	2012	2016
Cosenza	Natale	MA	Assault	12 to 20 years	2002	2017
Cotton	Ronald	NC	Sexual Assault	Life	1985	1995

119

Last Name	First Name	State	Crime	Sentence	Convicted	Exonerated
Courteau	Paul	RI	Robbery	15 years	1981	1999
Courtney	Sedrick	OK	Robbery	30 years	1996	2012
Courtney	Uriah	CA	Sexual Assault	Life	2006	2013
Cousin	Shareef	LA	Murder	Death	1996	1999
Cowans	Stephan	MA	Attempted Murder	30 to 45 years	1998	2004
Cox	Jeffrey	VA	Murder	Life	1991	2001
Credell	Cory	SC	Murder	Life	2001	2012
Cromedy	McKinley	NJ	Sexual Assault	60 years	1994	1999
Crotzer	Alan	FL	Sexual Assault	Life	1982	2006
Cruz	Efren	CA	Murder	41 to Life	1997	2001
Cuevas	Roberto	CA	Robbery	12 years	2003	2008
Cullipher	Ricky	VA	Assault	9 years	1997	2001
Cunningham	Calvin Wayne	VA	Sexual Assault	16 years	1981	2011
Curry	Martiece	MI	Sexual Assault	10 to 40 years	1990	1995
Czubryt	Robert	MA	Sexual Assault	2 months	2010	2016
Dabbs	Charles	NY	Sexual Assault	12 1/2 to 20 years	1984	1991
Dail	Dwayne Allen	NC	Child Sex Abuse	Life	1989	2007
Dake	Jeffrey	WI	Child Sex Abuse	16 years	1998	2007
Daniels	Elmer	DE	Child Sex Abuse	Life	1980	2018
Daniels	Erick	NC	Robbery	10 to 14 years	2001	2008
Davidson	Willie	VA	Sexual Assault	20 years	1981	2005
Davis	Cody	FL	Robbery	3 years	2006	2007
Davis	Donya	MI	Sexual Assault	22 years	2007	2014
Davis	Larry	WA	Sexual Assault	20 years and 6 months	1993	2010
Day	Lee Antione	IL	Murder	60 years	1992	2002
Daye	Frederick Renee	CA	Sexual Assault	Life	1984	1994
Deckinga	Shaun	F-MN	Robbery	10 years	1993	1993
Dedge	Wilton	FL	Sexual Assault	30 years	1982	2004
Denny	Mark	NY	Sexual Assault	19 to 57 years	1989	2017
Dewitt	Steven	DC	Murder	15 to Life	1992	2004
Diamond	Garry	VA	Sexual Assault	15 years	1977	2013
Diaz	Luis	FL	Sexual Assault	Life	1980	2005
Diaz	Luis	CA	Sexual Assault	15 years	1984	2012

120

Last Name	First Name	State	Crime	Sentence	Convicted	Exonerated
Dillon	William	FL	Murder	Life	1981	2008
Dixon	John	NJ	Sexual Assault	45 years	1991	2001
Dixon	Valentino	NY	Murder	38 1/3 to life	1992	2018
Dombrowski	Peter	NY	Robbery	9 to 18 years	1985	1990
Domenech	Alfredo	PA	Murder	Life	1988	2005
Dominguez	Alejandro	IL	Sexual Assault	9 years	1990	2002
Donald	Willie	IN	Murder	60 years	1992	2016
Dorval	Jean	NJ	Murder	60 years	1996	2018
Doswell	Thomas	PA	Sexual Assault	13 to 26 years	1986	2005
Dowaliby	David	IL	Murder	45 years	1990	1992
Drumgold	Shawn	MA	Murder	Life	1989	2003
Dubbs	Charles T.	PA	Sexual Assault	12 to 40 years	2002	2007
Dudley	Ronald	NY	Assault	15 years	2000	2001
Dupree, Jr.	Cornelius	TX	Robbery	75 years	1980	2011
Durham	Timothy	OK	Child Sex Abuse	Life	1993	1997
Dwight	Nathan Christopher	GA	Robbery	Life	2010	2013
Echavarria	Angel	MA	Murder	Life without parole	1996	2015
Echols	Douglas	GA	Sexual Assault	31 years	1987	2002
Elkins	Clarence	OH	Murder	55 to Life	1999	2005
Ellington	Tyrone	OH	Child Sex Abuse	Life	1989	1991
Ellis	Sean	MA	Murder	Life	1995	2018
Embry	Anthony	AL	Murder	20 years	1993	1997
Ennis	Sean	OH	Sexual Assault	5 to 25 years	1990	1994
Epps	Cory	NY	Murder	25 to life	1998	2017
Erby	Lonnie	MO	Child Sex Abuse	Life	1986	2003
Escalera	Robert	NY	Murder	15 to Life	1976	1990
Evans	Jerry Lee	TX	Sexual Assault	Life	1987	2009
Evans	Michael	IL	Murder	Life	1976	2003
Fappiano	Scott	NY	Sexual Assault	20 to 50 years	1985	2006
Fears, Jr.	Joseph R.	OH	Sexual Assault	15 to 25 years	1984	2009
Felder	Lance	PA	Murder	Life	1998	2014
Felix	Darren	NY	Attempted Murder	12 years	2004	2010
Fernandez	Pablo	NY	Murder	25 to life	1996	2019
Finch	Charles	NC	Murder	Death	1976	2019

121

Last Name	First Name	State	Crime	Sentence	Convicted	Exonerated
Flores, Jr.	Ernesto	TX	Burglary/Unlawful Entry	2 years	2004	2015
Foley	Kenneth Wayne	CA	Robbery	25 to Life	1995	2007
Foster	Demetrius	MI	Murder	32 to 50 years	2000	2014
Fountain	Wiley	TX	Sexual Assault	40 years	1986	2003
Fowler	Lawrence	NY	Murder	25 to Life	1998	2006
Frazier	Bryan	MA	Possession of Stolen Property	2 years and 6 months	2004	2009
Frese	George	AK	Murder	40 years	1999	2015
Frey	Joseph	WI	Sexual Assault	Life	1994	2013
Fritz	Judith	PA	Manslaughter	3 years	1995	1997
Fuller	Larry	TX	Sexual Assault	50 years	1981	2006
Fulmore	James	PA	Attempted Murder	15 to 30 years	2013	2016
Futrell	Rayshard	MI	Murder	Life	2009	2010
Gaines	Freddie Lee	AL	Murder	30 years	1974	1991
Galloway	Josiah	NY	Attempted Murder	25 years	2009	2018
Gantt	Timothy	CA	Murder	Life without parole	1994	2008
Garner	Terence	NC	Attempted Murder	32 to 43 years	1998	2002
Garry	Edward	NY	Murder	25 to life	1997	2018
Gatling	Paul	NY	Murder	30 to life	1964	2016
Giles	James Curtis	TX	Sexual Assault	30 years	1983	2007
Gillard	Larry	IL	Sexual Assault	24 years	1982	2009
Gillispie	Roger Dean	OH	Sexual Assault	22 to 56 years	1991	2017
Gilyard	Eugene	PA	Murder	Life	1998	2014
Glenn	Eugene	WI	Robbery	20 years	2002	2003
Glenn	Roosevelt	IN	Sexual Assault	36 years	1993	2017
Godschalk	Bruce	PA	Sexual Assault	10 to 20 years	1987	2002
Goldstein	Thomas Lee	CA	Murder	25 to Life	1980	2004
Gomez	Alfonso	CA	Murder	41 to Life	1998	2012
Gonzales-Barboza	Juan Carlos	KY	Child Sex Abuse	5 years	1996	2017
Gonzalez	Angel	IL	Sexual Assault	55 years	1995	2015
Gonzalez	Hector	NY	Murder	15 to Life	1996	2002
Good	Donald Wayne	TX	Sexual Assault	Life	1984	2004
Goodman	Bruce Dallas	UT	Murder	5 to Life	1986	2004
Goodman	Warren	WI	Robbery	22 years	1994	2007

122

Last Name	First Name	State	Crime	Sentence	Convicted	Exonerated
Goods	Darron	MD	Attempted Murder	Not sentenced	2005	2006
Gossett	Andrew	TX	Sexual Assault	50 years	2000	2007
Goudy	Walter	IN	Murder	110 years	1995	2012
Grajeda	Arthur	CA	Murder	32 to life	1987	1991
Grajeda	Senon	CA	Murder	45 to life	1987	1993
Gray	Adam	IL	Murder	Life without parole	1996	2017
Gray	David A.	IL	Attempted Murder	60 years	1978	1999
Gray	Paula	IL	Murder	50 years	1978	2002
Gray	Russell Leroy	VA	Murder	52 years	1987	1990
Green	Anthony Michael	OH	Sexual Assault	20 to 50 years	1988	2001
Green	Edward	DC	Sexual Assault	Not sentenced	1989	1990
Green	Kevin Lee	CA	Murder	15 to Life	1980	1996
Green	Michael Anthony	TX	Sexual Assault	75 years	1983	2010
Greene	Cy	NY	Murder	15 to life	1985	2006
Gregory	William	KY	Sexual Assault	70 years	1993	2000
Grimes	Don	AL	Robbery	Life without parole	1987	1996
Grimes	Willie	NC	Sexual Assault	Life	1988	2012
Groce	Tyrone	NY	Robbery	4 to 12 years	1993	1995
Guillory	Lavont	CA	Murder	Life	1994	2005
Gurley	Timothy	AL	Attempted Murder	35 years	2000	2002
Guzman	Humberto	MA	Drug Possession or Sale	18 to 20 years	1992	1997
Hale	Marshall	PA	Child Sex Abuse	23 1/2 to 47 years	1984	2017
Hammons	Robert	LA	Robbery	40 years	1986	1992
Hampton	Patrick	IL	Sexual Assault	60 years	1982	2011
Harding	Christopher	MA	Assault	10 to 12 years	1990	1998
Hargrave	Rosean	NY	Murder	30 to life	1992	2018
Harper	James	TN	Assault	5 years	1985	2005
Harper	Lafayette	IL	Murder	65 years	2014	2019
Harrell	Dion	NJ	Sexual Assault	8 years	1992	2016
Harris	Gerald	NY	Robbery	9 to 18 years	1992	2000
Harris	Keith	IL	Attempted Murder	50 years	1979	2003
Harris	William	WV	Sexual Assault	10 to 20 years	1987	1995
Harrison	Clarence	GA	Sexual Assault	Life	1987	2004

123

Last Name	First Name	State	Crime	Sentence	Convicted	Exonerated
Harward	Keith	VA	Murder	Life	1983	2016
Hatchett	Nathaniel	MI	Sexual Assault	25 to 40 years	1998	2008
Hayes	Reginald	NV	Murder	Life without parole	1985	1999
Haygood	Andre	TX	Murder	Life	2002	2011
Haynesworth	Thomas	VA	Sexual Assault	74 years	1984	2011
Henton	Eugene	TX	Sexual Assault	4 years	1984	2006
Herrera	Bobby Paiste	CA	Assault	5 years	1998	2000
Herrera	Moses	TX	Attempted Murder	7 years	1990	1992
Hicks	Anthony	WI	Sexual Assault	19 years	1991	1997
Hicks	Tyrone	NY	Sexual Assault	8 years	2000	2014
Hidalgo	Olmedo	NY	Murder	25 to Life	1992	2005
Highers	Raymond	MI	Murder	Life without parole	1988	2013
Highers	Thomas	MI	Murder	Life without parole	1988	2013
Hill	Darrin	LA	Sexual Assault	Committed to mental hospital	1999	2012
Hill	Dartangnan	OH	Kidnapping	24 years	2001	2005
Hill	James	IN	Sexual Assault	35 years	1982	2009
Hinton	Anthony	AL	Murder	Death	1986	2015
Hobley	Madison	IL	Murder	Death	1990	2003
Holdren	Larry	WV	Sexual Assault	30 to 60 years	1984	2000
Holemon	Jeffrey	AL	Sexual Assault	Life	1988	1999
Holland	Dana	IL	Sexual Assault	90 years	1997	2003
Holloway	Daryl	WI	Sexual Assault	Life	1993	2016
Holton	Rudolph	FL	Murder	Death	1987	2003
Honaker	Edward	VA	Sexual Assault	Life	1985	1994
Hood	Tyrone	IL	Murder	75 years	1996	2015
Hopkins	Troy	VA	Murder	28 years	1990	2005
Horn	Vernon	CT	Murder	70 years	2000	2018
Houston	Elton	IL	Murder	35 years	1984	1989
Howard	DeAndre	CA	Murder	Life	2003	2013
Howard	Timothy	OH	Murder	Death	1977	2003
Hudson	Larry	LA	Murder	Death	1967	1993
Hugee	Larry Lane	MD	Robbery	25 years	2004	2013
Hunt	Darryl	NC	Murder	Life	1985	2004

124

Last Name	First Name	State	Crime	Sentence	Convicted	Exonerated
Hunt	Kenya	CA	Robbery	Not sentenced	1991	1991
Hunter	Darrell	CA	Murder	Life without parole	2000	2008
Hutchison	Leonard	TN	Assault	25 years	1985	2005
Iglesias	Geraldo	IL	Murder	35 years	1994	2019
Imafidon	Julius	IA	Other	Probation	2000	2002
Irby	Derius	OH	Robbery	Not sentenced	2016	2017
Jackson	Charles	OH	Murder	30 to life	1991	2019
Jackson	Ieliot	IL	Drug Possession or Sale	13 years	2010	2018
Jackson	Joseph	NY	Murder	25 to life	1997	2018
Jackson	Marquis	CT	Murder	45 years	2000	2018
Jackson	Raymond	TX	Sexual Assault	Life	1984	2012
Jackson	Willie	LA	Sexual Assault	40 years	1989	2006
James	Gary Lamar	OH	Murder	Death	1977	2003
James	Henry	LA	Sexual Assault	Life without parole	1982	2011
Jardine	Alvin	HI	Sexual Assault	35 years	1992	2011
Jean	Lesly	NC	Sexual Assault	Life	1982	1991
Jenkins	Jerry Lee	MD	Sexual Assault	Life	1987	2013
Jernigan	Rachel	AZ	Robbery	14 years	2001	2008
Jimenez	Thaddeus	IL	Murder	50 years	1994	2009
Jimerson	Verneal	IL	Murder	Death	1985	1996
Johnson	Albert K.	CA	Sexual Assault	24 years	1992	2002
Johnson	Anthony	LA	Murder	Life	1986	2010
Johnson	Arthur	MS	Sexual Assault	55 years	1993	2008
Johnson	Calvin	GA	Sexual Assault	Life	1983	1999
Johnson	Chad	IL	Murder	80 years	2009	2018
Johnson	Charles	IL	Murder	Life without parole	1998	2017
Johnson	Donnell	MA	Murder	18 to 20 years	1996	2000
Johnson	Eugene	OH	Murder	18 to life	1996	2016
Johnson	Lamar	MD	Murder	Life	2005	2017
Johnson	Larry	MO	Sexual Assault	Life	1984	2002
Johnson	Latisha	NY	Attempted Murder	40 years	2007	2014
Johnson	Nathaniel	NY	Robbery	5 years	2010	2013
Johnson	Richard	IL	Sexual Assault	36 years	1992	1996

Last Name	First Name	State	Crime	Sentence	Convicted	Exonerated
Johnson	Rickey	LA	Sexual Assault	Life without parole	1983	2008
Johnston	Dale	OH	Murder	Death	1984	1990
Jones	Clifford	NY	Murder	18 to life	1981	2016
Jones	Darrell	MA	Murder	Life without parole	1986	2019
Jones	Dewey	OH	Murder	Life	1995	2014
Jones	Jeremiah	WA	Assault	Not sentenced	2001	2002
Jones	Joe C.	KS	Sexual Assault	Life	1986	1992
Jones	Michael	DC	Sexual Assault	9 to 30 years	1996	2019
Jones	Morris S.	TX	Assault	15 years	1998	2001
Jones	Richard	KS	Robbery	19 years	2001	2017
Jones	Robert	LA	Sexual Assault	Life without parole	1996	2017
Jones	Ronald	IL	Murder	Death	1989	1999
Jones	Tyrone	MD	Murder	Life	1999	2010
Jones	Wilbert	LA	Sexual Assault	Life	1973	2018
Joseph	Malenne	FL	Destruction of Property	Not sentenced	2010	2010
Kagonyera	Kenneth	NC	Murder	12 to 15 years	2001	2011
Kelly, Jr.	William M.	PA	Murder	10 to 20 years	1990	1993
Kezer	Joshua	MO	Murder	60 years	1994	2009
Kidd	Ricky	MO	Murder	Life without parole	1997	2019
Kimsey	Martin	TX	Robbery	Life	1985	1990
Kindle	Jason	CA	Robbery	70 to Life	2000	2003
Kirkwood	Justin	PA	Robbery	3 1/2 to 7 years	2003	2006
Kotler	Kerry	NY	Sexual Assault	25 to 50 years	1982	1992
Kussmaul	Richard	TX	Murder	Life without parole	1994	2019
Kyles	Curtis	LA	Murder	Death	1984	1998
Larkin	Francis	F-WI	Robbery	32 years and 6 months	1991	1999
Larsen	Daniel	CA	Other Nonviolent Felony	28 to life	1999	2014
Lavernia	Carlos Marcos	TX	Sexual Assault	Life	1985	2000
Lawson	Samuel	OR	Murder	Life	2005	2014
Lee	Ah	PA	Murder	Life	1988	2004
Lee	Ralph	NJ	Murder	Life	1996	2018
Leka	Sami	NY	Murder	20 years	1990	2002

Last Name	First Name	State	Crime	Sentence	Convicted	Exonerated
Lemus	David	NY	Murder	25 to Life	1992	2007
Letemps	Jules	FL	Sexual Assault	Life	1989	2016
Leverett	Ron	GA	Drug Possession or Sale	3 years	1993	1994
Lewis	George	MN	Sexual Assault	12 years and 8 months	1988	1991
Lewis	Terrance	PA	Murder	Life without parole	1999	2019
Lindsey	Johnnie	TX	Sexual Assault	Life	1983	2009
Logan	Alton	IL	Murder	Life	1982	2008
Logan	Roger	NY	Murder	25 to life	1999	2014
Lomax	Walter	MD	Murder	Life	1968	2014
Long	James	TX	Sexual Assault	20 years	1994	2019
Long	Lee	NY	Sexual Assault	8 to 24 years	1995	2002
Lopez	George	CA	Robbery	13 years	2000	2002
Love	Dwight	MI	Murder	Life	1982	2001
Lyons	Marcus	IL	Sexual Assault	6 years	1988	2007
Madrigal	Rafael	CA	Attempted Murder	53 to Life	2002	2009
Mahan	Dale	AL	Sexual Assault	35 years	1986	1998
Mahan	Ronnie	AL	Sexual Assault	Life without parole	1986	1998
Maher	Dennis	MA	Sexual Assault	Life	1984	2003
Maldonado	Robert	NY	Attempted Murder	8 to 16 years	1998	2004
Marshall	Michael	GA	Robbery	4 years	2008	2009
Martin	Wayne	NY	Murder	Life without parole	2010	2016
Martinez	Angelo	NY	Murder	25 to Life	1986	2002
Martinez	Benny	NM	Murder	20 years	1998	2001
Martinez Jr.	Ruben	CA	Robbery	40 years and 8 months	2008	2019
Mason	Terrence	NY	Robbery	10 to 20 years	1987	1995
Massey	Shawn Giovanni	NC	Kidnapping	11 1/2 to 15 1/4 years	1999	2010
Massingill	Anthony	TX	Robbery	Life	1980	2014
Masterson	Kerry	IL	Murder	58 years	2011	2017
Matthews	Ryan	LA	Murder	Death	1999	2004
Mayes	Larry	IN	Sexual Assault	80 years	1982	2001
McAlister	Michael	VA	Sexual Assault	35 years	1986	2015
McCaughn	Patrick	IL	Robbery	12 years	1996	1999

Last Name	First Name	State	Crime	Sentence	Convicted	Exonerated
McClendon	Robert	OH	Child Sex Abuse	15 to Life	1991	2008
McCord	Todd	NY	Murder	25 to life	1987	1994
McCullough	Jack	IL	Murder	Life	2012	2016
McGee	Arvin	OK	Sexual Assault	Life	1989	2002
McGee	Leroy	FL	Robbery	4 years and 6 months	1991	1995
McGowan	Thomas	TX	Sexual Assault	Life	1985	2008
McHenry	Marwin	MI	Attempted Murder	16 to 27 years	2013	2017
McIntyre	Lamonte	KS	Murder	Life	1994	2017
McKay	Cornell	MO	Robbery	12 years	2013	2015
McKee	Larry	NY	Murder	24 to life	1997	2018
McKinney	DeWayne	CA	Murder	Life	1981	2000
McKinney	Lawrence	TN	Sexual Assault	100 years	1978	2009
McMillan	Clark Jerome	TN	Sexual Assault	Life	1980	2002
McNary	Willie Earl	CA	Assault	11 years and 8 months	1984	1996
McSherry	Leonard	CA	Child Sex Abuse	48 years	1988	2001
Medina	Alarico Joe	CO	Murder	Life	1991	1995
Mercer	Michael	NY	Sexual Assault	21 to 41 years	1992	2003
Mervilus	Emmanuel	NJ	Robbery	11 years	2008	2013
Milla	Marco	CA	Murder	Life without parole	2002	2015
Miller	Billy Wayne	TX	Sexual Assault	Life	1984	2006
Miller	Christopher	OH	Sexual Assault	40 years	2002	2018
Miller	Harry	UT	Robbery	5 to Life	2004	2007
Miller	Jerry	IL	Sexual Assault	45 years	1982	2007
Miller	Morgan	OH	Robbery	20 to 40 years	1984	1992
Miller	Neil	MA	Sexual Assault	26 to 45 years	1990	2000
Miller, Jr.	Lawrence J.	CT	Assault	32 years	1983	1997
Mims	Bernard	IL	Murder	95 years	2006	2016
Mitchell	Marvin	MA	Child Sex Abuse	9 to 25 years	1990	1997
Mitchell	Perry	SC	Sexual Assault	30 years	1984	1998
Montalvo	Ruben	NY	Murder	15 to Life	1988	2001
Montgomery	Konrad	MI	Robbery	12 to 27 years	2013	2016
Montgomery	LaDondrell	TX	Robbery	Life	2010	2011
Moon	Brandon	TX	Sexual Assault	75 years	1988	2005

Last Name	First Name	State	Crime	Sentence	Convicted	Exonerated
Moore	Anthony	NY	Murder	25 to Life	1996	1999
Moore	Clarence	NJ	Sexual Assault	Life	1987	2006
Moore	Jonathan	IL	Murder	76 years	2002	2012
Moore	Joshua	CA	Robbery	12 years	1999	2001
Morales	Jose	NY	Murder	15 to Life	1988	2001
Moran	Nakiya	IL	Attempted Murder	62 years	2009	2017
Moses-EL	Clarence	CO	Sexual Assault	48 years	1988	2016
Moto	Vincent	PA	Sexual Assault	12 to 24 years	1987	1996
Munson	Adolph	OK	Murder	Death	1985	1995
Myers	Hubert	FL	Murder	Life	1976	2019
Nash	Alprentiss	IL	Murder	80 years	1997	2012
Neely	Todd	FL	Attempted Murder	15 years	1987	1989
Negron	Julio	NY	Attempted Murder	12 years	2006	2017
Nelson	Robert	MO	Sexual Assault	70 years	1984	2013
Nesmith	Willie James	PA	Sexual Assault	9 to 25 years	1982	2001
Newsome	James	IL	Murder	Life	1980	1995
Newton	Alan	NY	Sexual Assault	13 1/2 to 40 years	1985	2006
Nickerson	Glen	CA	Murder	Life without parole	1987	2003
Nieves	William	PA	Murder	Death	1994	2000
Nnodimele	Martin	NY	Robbery	10 years	2008	2012
Northrop	Alan	WA	Sexual Assault	23 years and 6 months	1993	2010
Norwood	Matthew	MS	Robbery	15 years	1997	2010
Ochoa	James	CA	Robbery	2 years	2005	2006
Odiase	Steven	NY	Murder	25 to life	2013	2017
Odom	Kirk	DC	Sexual Assault	20 to 66 years	1981	2012
O'Donnell	James	NY	Sexual Assault	3 1/2 to 7 years	1998	2000
Olebar	Brandon	WA	Robbery	16 years and 6 months	2003	2013
O'Loughlin	Kevin	MA	Child Sex Abuse	4 to 6 years	1983	2015
O'Neal	Johnnie	NY	Sexual Assault	10 to 20 years	1985	2013
Ortiz	Armando Rodriguez	CA	Murder	Life	2003	2007
Ortiz	Victor	NY	Sexual Assault	12 1/2 to 25 years	1984	1996
Pacyon	Douglas	NY	Sexual Assault	3 years and 6 months	1985	2010

Last Name	First Name	State	Crime	Sentence	Convicted	Exonerated
Pallares	Jose	CA	Weapon Possession or Sale	2 years	2005	2008
Palmer	Lamar	NY	Assault	9 years	2000	2001
Parish	Christopher	IN	Attempted Murder	30 years	1998	2006
Passley	Marlon	MA	Murder	Life	1996	2000
Patterson	Dontia	PA	Murder	Life without parole	2009	2018
Patterson	Maurice	IL	Murder	30 years	2003	2010
Peacock	Freddie	NY	Sexual Assault	5 years	1976	2010
Pease	Kevin	AK	Murder	60 years	1999	2015
Pejcinovic	Adam	NY	Assault	3 to 9 years	1988	1993
Pejcinovic	Frank	NY	Assault	1 to 3 years	1989	1993
Pendleton	Marlon	IL	Sexual Assault	20 years	1996	2006
Peralta	David	GA	Murder	Life	2001	2013
Perez	Jose	CA	Robbery	13 years	2012	2019
Perez	Richard	CA	Robbery	Not sentenced	2001	2001
Persad	Vishnu	FL	Assault	43 years	2001	2007
Peterson	Kevin K.	NE	Murder	Not sentenced	1994	1995
Pettiford	Antoine	MD	Murder	Life	1995	2000
Phillips	Michael	TX	Sexual Assault	12 years	1990	2014
Phillips	Steven	TX	Sexual Assault	40 years	1982	2008
Pierce	Jeffrey Todd	OK	Sexual Assault	65 years	1986	2001
Pierre	Charles	NY	Murder	25 to life	2003	2015
Pierre	Duquene	NJ	Murder	60 years	1996	2016
Pinchback	Johnny	TX	Child Sex Abuse	Life	1984	2011
Pinkins	Darryl	IN	Sexual Assault	65 years	1991	2016
Piszczek	Brian	OH	Sexual Assault	15 to 25 years	1991	1994
Pitts, Jr.	James	TX	Sexual Assault	20 years	1994	2019
Polonia	Diomedes	NY	Attempted Murder	14 to 18 years	1998	2003
Pondexter	Ronald	NY	Murder	25 to life	1993	1997
Pope	David Shawn	TX	Sexual Assault	45 years	1986	2001
Porter	Allen Wayne	TX	Sexual Assault	Life	1991	2010
Porter	Anthony	IL	Murder	Death	1983	1999
Porter	Kerry	KY	Murder	60 years	1998	2011
Porter	Michael	FL	Sexual Assault	Life	1988	2002
Powell	Anthony	MA	Sexual Assault	12 to 20 years	1992	2004

130

Last Name	First Name	State	Crime	Sentence	Convicted	Exonerated
Prati, Jr.	Ronald	NJ	Sexual Assault	20 years	1996	2009
Pratt	Elmer	CA	Murder	25 to Life	1972	1999
Prentice	Mark	NY	Robbery	12 1/2 to 25 years	1989	1995
Quindt	David	CA	Murder	Not sentenced	1999	2000
Raby, Jr.	Earl	MI	Destruction of Property	Probation	1998	1999
Rachell	Ricardo	TX	Child Sex Abuse	40 years	2003	2011
Radillo, Jr.	Sergio	FL	Attempted Murder	Life	1995	2005
Rainge	Willie	IL	Murder	Life	1978	1996
Ramchair	Racky	NY	Robbery	10 to 20 years	1997	2010
Ramirez	Jesus	TX	Murder	Life	1998	2008
Randolph	Guy	MA	Child Sex Abuse	10 years	1991	2008
Ranta	David	NY	Murder	37 1/2 to Life	1991	2013
Reed	Cornelius	WI	Murder	Life	1993	1997
Reed	Deshawn	CA	Murder	Life without parole	2014	2017
Register	Kash	CA	Murder	Life without parole	1979	2013
Reichert	Joseph	WA	Robbery	Not sentenced	2001	2003
Reid	Mark	CT	Sexual Assault	12 years	1997	2003
Reynolds	Donald	IL	Sexual Assault	69 years	1988	1997
Richardson	Dietrich	IL	Robbery	30 years	2011	2016
Rivera	Jacques	IL	Murder	80 years	1990	2011
Rivera	Jonathan	PR	Murder	Life	2007	2008
Rivera	Juan	IL	Murder	Life	1993	2012
Roberts	Larry Trent	PA	Murder	Life without parole	2007	2019
Roberts	Marvin	AK	Murder	33 years	1999	2015
Roberts	Rodney	NJ	Kidnapping	7 years	1996	2014
Robertson	Shakara	TX	Robbery	Probation	1996	2012
Robinson	Anthony	TX	Sexual Assault	27 years	1987	2000
Robles	Willie	CA	Robbery	Not sentenced	1991	1991
Rocha	Mario	CA	Murder	35 to Life	1998	2008
Rodrigues	Shaun	HI	Kidnapping	20 years	2002	2014
Rodriguez	George	TX	Child Sex Abuse	60 years	1987	2005
Rodriguez	Jeffrey	CA	Robbery	25 to Life	2003	2007
Rodriguez	Jose	NY	Robbery	10 years	2007	2011

131

Last Name	First Name	State	Crime	Sentence	Convicted	Exonerated
Rodriguez	Ricardo	IL	Murder	90 years	1997	2018
Rogers	Mandel	TX	Robbery	12 years	1999	2014
Rojas	Luis Kevin	NY	Murder	15 to Life	1992	1998
Rollins	Donte	PA	Attempted Murder	62 1/2 to 125 years	2007	2016
Rollins	Lafonso	IL	Sexual Assault	75 years	1994	2004
Rollins, IV	Offord	CA	Murder	29 to life	1992	1996
Rosario	Richard	NY	Murder	25 to life	1998	2016
Rose	Peter	CA	Child Sex Abuse	27 years	1995	2005
Ruano	Julio	LA	Assault	7 years	2011	2017
Rubalcava	Lionel	CA	Attempted Murder	31 to Life	2003	2019
Ruffin	Julius	VA	Sexual Assault	Life	1982	2003
Russell	Stephen Lynn	TX	Robbery	50 years	1980	1990
Ryan	Michael	NJ	Other	Probation	2016	2018
Sailor	Ru-El	OH	Murder	25 to life	2003	2018
Salazar	Ben	TX	Sexual Assault	30 years	1992	1997
Salley	MarQuise	PA	Murder	Life without parole	2010	2019
Salter	Aaron	MI	Murder	Life without parole	2003	2018
Sanchez	Isauro	IL	Murder	Life without parole	1982	1991
Sanders	David	WI	Child Sex Abuse	15 years	2006	2007
Sanders	Rodell	IL	Murder	80 years	1995	2014
Santos	Louis	MA	Murder	Life	1985	1990
Sarsfield	Eric	MA	Sexual Assault	10 to 15 years	1987	2000
Sawyer	Thomas	MI	Sexual Assault	22 to 32 years	1992	2003
Schand	Mark	MA	Murder	Life without parole	1987	2013
Scheidell	Daniel	WI	Sexual Assault	25 years	1995	2017
Schulz	Stephen	NY	Robbery	11 years	1999	2009
Scott	Christopher Shun	TX	Murder	Life	1997	2009
Scott	Samuel	GA	Sexual Assault	Life	1987	2002
Scott	Scotty	AR	Murder	25 years	1983	1989
Scott	Winston	VA	Sexual Assault	14 years	1976	2019
Scruggs	Dwayne D.	IN	Sexual Assault	40 years	1986	1993
Sealie	Frank	AL	Murder	Life without parole	2014	2015

Last Name	First Name	State	Crime	Sentence	Convicted	Exonerated
Seiber	George	OH	Assault	10 to 25 years	1987	1999
Seri	Michael Caesar	CT	Child Sex Abuse	6 months to 5 years	2001	2003
Sermeno	Miguel Angel	CA	Traffic Offense	8 months	1995	1997
Serrano	Ivan	PA	Murder	Life	1988	2005
Shannon	Michael	LA	Murder	Life without parole	2011	2018
Shaughnessy	Eric	MA	Assault	5 years	1997	1998
Shelton	Horace	NC	Forgery	10 7/12 to 13 1/2 years	2012	2014
Shelton	Michael	TX	Sexual Assault	20 years	2014	2019
Shephard	David L.	NJ	Sexual Assault	30 years	1984	1995
Shomberg	Forest	WI	Sexual Assault	12 years	2003	2009
Showers	Kurtis DeAngelo	MI	Robbery	Life	1994	1998
Shull	George Edward	CA	Sexual Assault	5 years	1989	2009
Sierra	Thomas	IL	Murder	55 years	1997	2018
Sifuentes	Alberto	TX	Murder	Life	1998	2008
Siggers	Darrell	MI	Murder	Life without parole	1984	2018
Silva-Santiago	Jesus	MA	Murder	Life without parole	2006	2010
Simmons III	Tommy	CA	Murder	Life	1998	2003
Simmons, Jr.	Claude	TX	Murder	Life	1997	2009
Sims	Lennie Darrold	CA	Robbery	7 years	1992	1994
Sims	Mack	IN	Attempted Murder	35 years	1994	2019
Sinegal	Layo	AK	Sexual Assault	5 years	1995	2000
Slater	Willie Lee	FL	Assault	Life	1999	2009
Smith	Alonzo	IL	Murder	40 years	1984	2015
Smith	Billy James	TX	Sexual Assault	Life	1987	2006
Smith	Frank Lee	FL	Murder	Death	1986	2000
Smith	Julius	NJ	Robbery	20 years	2010	2017
Smith	Marcus Lashun	TX	Robbery	Probation	1995	2012
Smith	Michael	CA	Murder	Life without parole	1994	2009
Smith	Walter D.	OH	Sexual Assault	78 to Life	1986	1996
Snipes	Steven	NC	Robbery	7 years and 6 months	1998	2003
Snyder	Walter	VA	Sexual Assault	45 years	1986	1993
Sonnier	Ernest	TX	Kidnapping	Life	1986	2018

Last Name	First Name	State	Crime	Sentence	Convicted	Exonerated
Steese	Fred	NV	Murder	Life without parole	1995	2017
Stevens	Richard	F-NJ	Sexual Assault	14 years	1990	1992
Stewart	Arthur	NY	Robbery	7 to 14 years	1995	2001
Stewart	Kia	LA	Murder	Life without parole	2009	2015
Stewart	Ronald	FL	Murder	50 years	1985	2019
Strickland	Reshenda	WA	Robbery	6 months	2004	2004
Sturgeon	Richard	TX	Robbery	50 years	1999	2009
Styles	Larod	IL	Murder	Life without parole	1998	2017
Sutherlin	David Brian	MN	Sexual Assault	3 years and 7 months	1985	2002
Sutton	Josiah	TX	Sexual Assault	25 years	1999	2004
Swift	Walter	MI	Sexual Assault	30 to 55 years	1982	2008
Talamantez	Jesse	TX	Murder	99 years	1999	2004
Tall Bear	Johnny	OK	Murder	Life without parole	1992	2018
Talley	Dell	VA	Sexual Assault	Not sentenced	1991	1991
Taylor	Andre	CA	Attempted Murder	28 to life	1990	1998
Taylor	Rhian	NY	Murder	20 to life	2010	2017
Taylor	Ronald Gene	TX	Sexual Assault	60 years	1995	2008
Terry	Paul	IL	Murder	Life	1977	2003
Thibodeaux	Damon	LA	Murder	Death	1997	2012
Thomas	Deama	IN	Robbery	6 years	1989	1992
Thomas	Rickey Dale	TX	Robbery	Life	1992	1993
Thomas	Victor Larue	TX	Sexual Assault	Life	1986	2001
Thompson	Grover	IL	Attempted Murder	40 years	1981	2019
Thompson	Hubert	CT	Sexual Assault	12 years	1998	2012
Thompson	John	LA	Murder	Death	1985	2003
Thompson	John	LA	Robbery	49 years and 6 months	1985	1999
Thompson	Luqris	NV	Kidnapping	9 to 23 years	2007	2012
Thompson	Teddy	VA	Robbery	16 years	2001	2007
Thorpe	Dwayne	PA	Murder	Life	2009	2019
Thurman	Philip Leon	VA	Sexual Assault	31 years	1985	2005
Tillman	James Calvin	CT	Sexual Assault	45 years	1989	2006
Tingle, Jr.	John	VA	Assault	10 years	1993	1994

134

Last Name	First Name	State	Crime	Sentence	Convicted	Exonerated
Tomlin	Charles	CA	Murder	25 to life	1979	1994
Toney	Steven	MO	Sexual Assault	Life	1983	1996
Torres	Alfredo	F-NM	Drug Possession or Sale	5 years and 10 months	2006	2009
Towler	Raymond	OH	Child Sex Abuse	Life	1981	2010
Trevino	Michael	TX	Child Sex Abuse	Probation	1993	2012
Trulove	Jamal	CA	Murder	50 to life	2010	2015
Tucker	David	MI	Assault	6 to 10 years	1992	1999
Turner	Keith	TX	Sexual Assault	20 years	1983	2005
Turner	Kenneth	CA	Murder	Not sentenced	1995	1995
Uriostegui	Silvano	TX	Assault	Not sentenced	2012	2012
Vamvakas	Evangelo	NY	Robbery	3 1/2 to 10 years	1994	1996
Varela	Ignacio	IL	Murder	Life without parole	1982	1991
Varela	Joaquin	IL	Murder	Life without parole	1982	1991
Vargas	Luis	CA	Sexual Assault	55 years	1999	2015
Vasquez	David	VA	Murder	35 years	1985	1989
Vasquez	Mario	WI	Child Sex Abuse	20 years	1998	2015
Vazquez	Hector	F-TX	Drug Possession or Sale	Not sentenced	2004	2005
Veasy	Willie	PA	Murder	Life without parole	1993	2019
Velasquez	Eduardo	MA	Sexual Assault	12 to 18 years	1988	2001
Velez	John	IL	Murder	55 years	2002	2017
Vent	Eugene	AK	Murder	38 years	1999	2015
Vera	Francisco	IL	Assault	17 years	1992	1998
Vera	John	NY	Robbery	6 to 18 years	1995	2000
Virgil	William	KY	Murder	70 years	1988	2017
VonAllmen	Michael	KY	Sexual Assault	35 years	1982	2010
Walker	James	NY	Murder	20 to Life	1971	1990
Walker	Joseph	SC	Sexual Assault	24 years	2003	2014
Walker	William	OH	Robbery	3 years	2002	2005
Waller	James	TX	Child Sex Abuse	30 years	1983	2007
Waller	Patrick	TX	Kidnapping	Life	1992	2008
Wallis	Gregory	TX	Sexual Assault	50 years	1989	2007
Wanzer	Terry Lee	GA	Sexual Assault	Life	1973	1991
Ward	Bernard	MD	Murder	Life	1989	1994

Last Name	First Name	State	Crime	Sentence	Convicted	Exonerated
Ward	Nathaniel	TX	Robbery	45 years	1999	2001
Wardell	Billy	IL	Sexual Assault	69 years	1988	1997
Warner	Colin	NY	Murder	15 to Life	1982	2001
Washington	Darryl	TX	Robbery	Life	1996	2012
Washington	Michael	WA	Burglary/Unlawful Entry	1 year	2005	2006
Washington	Vonaire	WI	Robbery	22 years	1991	2001
Waters	Leo	NC	Sexual Assault	Life	1982	2003
Watkins	John	AZ	Sexual Assault	14 years	2004	2010
Ways	Anthony	NJ	Murder	Life	1991	2005
Weatherly	Harold	OK	Attempted Murder	40 years	1984	2007
Webb	Mark	TX	Sexual Assault	30 years	1987	2002
Webb	Troy	VA	Sexual Assault	47 years	1989	1996
Webb, III	Thomas	OK	Sexual Assault	60 years	1983	1996
Webster	Bernard	MD	Sexual Assault	30 years	1983	2002
Weichel	Fred	MA	Murder	Life without parole	1981	2017
Whitaker	Mark	PA	Murder	Life without parole	2003	2019
White	John Jerome	GA	Sexual Assault	Life	1980	2007
Whitfield	Arthur Lee	VA	Sexual Assault	63 years	1982	2009
Whitley	Drew	PA	Murder	Life	1989	2006
Wickham	Christopher	UT	Sexual Assault	20 to life	1997	2019
Wiggins	David Lee	TX	Child Sex Abuse	Life	1989	2012
Wilcox	George	AR	Assault	Not sentenced	1998	2001
Wilcoxson	Robert	NC	Murder	12 1/2 to 15 3/4 years	2002	2011
Wilhite	Charles	MA	Murder	Life	2010	2013
Wilkerson	Mike	MO	Sexual Assault	Committed to mental hospital	2000	2017
Williams	Archie	LA	Attempted Murder	Life without parole	1983	2019
Williams	Darrell	OK	Sexual Assault	Probation	2012	2014
Williams	Dennis	IL	Murder	Death	1978	1996
Williams	Derrick Raphel	FL	Sexual Assault	Life	1993	2011
Williams	Hubert	MD	Attempted Murder	100 years	1998	2009
Williams	James Curtis	TX	Sexual Assault	Life	1984	2012
Williams	Jerron	FL	Manslaughter	50 years	2013	2015

Last Name	First Name	State	Crime	Sentence	Convicted	Exonerated
Williams	Jimmy	OH	Child Sex Abuse	Life	1991	2001
Williams	Lawrence	NY	Assault	10 years	2009	2012
Williams	Michael Anthony	LA	Sexual Assault	Life without parole	1981	2005
Williams	Richard	CA	Murder	Life without parole	1998	2015
Williams	Willie	GA	Sexual Assault	45 years	1985	2007
Williams, Jr.	Clifford	FL	Murder	Death	1976	2019
Williams, Jr.	Johnny	CA	Child Sex Abuse	16 years	2000	2013
Williams, Jr.	Larry	NC	Murder	10 years	2002	2015
Willis	Calvin	LA	Child Sex Abuse	Life without parole	1982	2003
Willis	Cedric	MS	Murder	Life	1997	2006
Willis	John	IL	Sexual Assault	Life	1993	1999
Willis	Marrio D'Shane	OK	Robbery	10 years	2003	2006
Wilson	Andrew	CA	Murder	Life without parole	1986	2017
Wilson	Deontae	OH	Robbery	Not sentenced	2017	2017
Wilson	Robert	IL	Attempted Murder	30 years	1999	2006
Winston	Michael	IL	Murder	40 years	2007	2012
Winston	Michael	WI	Attempted Murder	26 years	2013	2018
Woodall	Glen	WV	Sexual Assault	Life	1987	1992
Woodard	James Lee	TX	Murder	Life	1981	2008
Woodley	Collin	NY	Drug Possession or Sale	10 to 20 years	1990	1998
Woods	Anthony	MO	Child Sex Abuse	25 years	1984	2005
Woten	Michael Anthony	TX	Robbery	55 years	1982	1990
Wurdemann	John	ID	Attempted Murder	Life	2002	2018
Wyatt	Rickey Dale	TX	Sexual Assault	99 years	1981	2012
Wyniemko	Kenneth	MI	Sexual Assault	40 to 60 years	1994	2003
Yarris	Nicholas	PA	Murder	Death	1982	2003
York	Kenneth	MO	Sexual Assault	Life without parole	1994	2010
Youngblood	Larry	AZ	Child Sex Abuse	10 years and 6 months	1985	2000
Zapata	Rodrigo	TX	Robbery	25 years	2000	2001

Bibliography

AB 648, Assembly Bill from the Wisconsin State Assembly, 2005.

"About the American Law Institute." Brochure, American Law Institute, http://www.ali.org/doc/thisIsALI.pdf.

Acker, J. R. & Lanier, C. S. "Law, Discretion, and the Capital Jury: death penalty statutes and proposals for reform." Criminal Law Bulletin, 1996. [*Note: the topic of this thesis was initially death penalty reform. As such, this background reading provided me with a great deal of insights into witness misidentification.]

Adams, Lucy. "Death by Discretion: Who Decides Who Lives and Dies in the United States of America?" American Journal of Criminal Law, vol. 32, no. 3, Summer 2005.

Amsterdam, Anthony. "Courtroom Contortions: How America's Application of the Death Penalty Erodes the Principle of Equal Justice Under Law." *The American Prospect*, July 2004.

Bedau, Hugo and Michael L. Radelet. "Miscarriages of Justice in Potentially Capital Cases." Stanford Law Review, vol. 40, 1987.

Berger. "Justice delayed or justice denied?—a comment on recent proposals to reform the death penalty habeas corpus." Columbia Law Review, 1990.

Berlow, Alan. "The Broken Machinery of Death." American Prospect, July 30, 2001.

Blecker, Robert. "Among Killers, Searching for the Worst of the Worst." The Washington Post, December 3, 2000.

Bottoson v. Moore, 833 So. 2d 693 (Fla. 2002).

Brady v. Maryland 373 U.S. 83 (1963).

Brooks, Richard and Stephen Raphael. "Life Terms or Death Sentences: The Uneasy Relationship Between Judicial Elections and Capital Punishment." The Journal of Law and Criminology, vol 92, 2003.

Burnside, Fred. "Dying to Get Elected: A Challenge to the Jury Override." Wisconsin Law Review, 1999.

California Criminal Jury Instructions. Section 105: Witnesses, Judicial Council of California, http://www2.courtinfo.ca.gov/crimjuryinst/, 2005.

California Penal Code § 859.7 (2018).

Clark. "Procedural Reforms in Capital Cases Applied to Perjury." The John Marshall Law Review, 2001.

Clements, Noah. "Flipping a Coin: A Solution for the Inherent Unreliability of Eyewitness Identification Testimony." Indiana Law Review, 2007.

Collins, Winn S. "Safeguards for Eyewitness Identification." *Wisconsin Lawyer*, March 2004.

Costanzo, Mark. "Just revenge: costs and consequences of the death penalty." St. Martin's Press, New York, 1997.

Coyle, Marcia, et al. "Fatal Defense: Trial and Error in the Nation's Death Belt." National Law Journal, June 11, 1990.

Crimestar. "Law Enforcement Record Management and Investigation System." http://www.crimestar.com/lineups.html.

"Deadly Disparities." The New York Times, September 17, 2000 (editorial).

"Death Penalty Sentencing: Research Indicates Pattern of Racial Disparities." U.S. General Accounting Office, 1990.

"Death Without Justice: A Guide for Examining the Administration of the Death Penalty in the United States." Ohio State Law Journal, 2002.

Dillickrath, Thomas. "Expert Testimony on Eyewitness Identification: Admissibility and Alternatives." University of Miami Law Review, July 2001.

Doyle, James M. "Two Stories of Eyewitness Error." The Champion, November 2003.

"Due Process and the Death Penalty in Illinois." Chicago Council of Lawyers, March 2000.

Ehlers, Scott. "Eyewitness Identification: State Law Reform." Champion, National Association of Criminal Defense Lawyers, April 2005.

"The Eighth Amendment and Ineffective Assistance of Counsel in Capital Trials." Harvard Law Review, vol 107, 1993–1994.

"Eligibility for Capital Punishment: Chapter 4." Illinois Commission on Capital Punishment, Final Report, April 15, 2002.

"Exonerated Death-Row Inmate Awarded $2.5 million." Jet, vol 109, no. 20, May 22, 2006.

Feige, David L. "I'll Never Forget that Face: The Science and Law of the Double-Blind Sequential Lineup." The Champion, January/February 2003.

Fisher, Stanley and Ian McKenzie. "A Miscarriage of Justice in Massachusetts: Eyewitness Identification Procedures, Unrecorded Admissions, and a Comparison with English Law." Boston University Public Interest Law Journal, Fall 2003.

Fisher, Stanley Z. "The Prosecutor's Ethical Duty to Seek Exculpatory Evidence in Police Hands: Lessons from England." Fordham Law Review, vol. 68, no. 5, April 2000.

"Fixing the Death Penalty." *Chicago Tribune*, December 29, 2000 (editorial).

"Florida Death Penalty Assessment Report." American Bar Association, http://www.abanet.org/media/releases/news091706.html, September 17, 2006.

Foglia, Wanda. "They Know Not What They Do: Unguided and Misguided Discretion in Pennsylvania Capital Cases." Justice Quarterly, vol. 20, no. 1, March 2003.

Forde-Mazrui, Kim. "Jural Districting: Selecting Impartial Juries Through Community Representation." Vanderbilt Law Review, vol. 52, no. 2, March 1999.

Gambell, Suzannah. "The Need to Revisit the *Neil v. Biggers* Factors: Suppressing Unreliable Eyewitness Identifications." Wyoming Law Review, 2006.

Geller. "Videotaping Interrogations and Confessions." National Institute of Justice, March 1993.

Gert, Heather. "The Death Penalty and Victims' Rights: Legal Advance Directives." Journal of Value Inquiry, vol. 33, no. 4, December 1999.

Grano, Joseph. "Kirby, Biggers, and Ash: Do Any Constitutional Safeguards Remain After the Danger of Convicting the Innocent?" Michigan Law Review, no. 72, 1974.

Greenhouse, Linda. "Justices Narrowly Resolve Dispute on Jury Instruction." *The New York Times*, January 20, 2000.

Gross, Samuel and Robert Mauro. "Death and Discrimination: Racial Disparities in Capital Sentencing." 1989.

Gross, Samuel R., et al. "Exonerations in the United States 1989 through 2003." Journal of Criminal Law and Criminology, vol. 95, no. 2, 2005.

Guccione, Jean. "Relief Coming for Jurors Ill at Ease with Legalese; A State Panel OKs Simple Civil Jury Instructions. Criminal Courts are Next." *Los Angeles Times*, July 18, 2003.

"The Guilt-Innocent Phase: Chapter 9." Illinois Commission on Capital Punishment, April 15, 2002.

Hanley, Robert. "Problems Abound in Picking Brink's Jury." *The New York Times*, July 19, 1983.

Harmon, Talia Roitberg. "Race for Your Life: An Analysis of the Role of Race in Erroneous Capital Convictions." Criminal Justice Review, vol. 29, Spring 2004.

HB 103, Chapter 590, House Bill from the Maryland State House, 2007.

HB 2632, House Bill from the Virginia State House, 2005.

Herbert, Bob. "Who Gets the Death Penalty?" *The New York Times*, May 13, 2002.

Himelstein, Shmuel, Rabbi, trans. *Mishnah*. Maor Wallach Press, 1994.

"How the Malfunctioning Death Penalty Challenges the Criminal Justice System." *Judicature* vol. 89, no. 5, March 2006.

Huff, R. C., et al. "Convicted but Innocent." Thousand Oaks, CA: Sage, 1996.

Illinois Commission on Capital Punishment, Final Report. April 15, 2002.

Jackson, Barbara. "Letter to the Editor: Re 'Say What, Your Honor?'" *Los Angeles Times*, September 13, 2000.

Jones. "Death Penalty Procedures: A Proposal for Reform." Texas Bar Journal, 1990.

Kan, Yee and Scott Phillips. "Race and the Death Penalty: Including Asian Americans and Exploring the Desocialization of Law." Journal of Ethnicity in Criminal Justice, vol. 1, no. 1, 2003.

Klobuchar, Amy and Hilary Lindell Caligiuri. "Protecting the Innocent/Convicting the Guilty: Hennepin County's Pilot Project in Blind Sequential Eyewitness Identification." William Mitchell Law Review, 2005.

Koch, Rudolf. "Process v. Outcome: The Proper Role of Corroborative Evidence in Due Process Analysis of Eyewitness Identification Testimony." Cornell Law Review, May 2003.

Koepell, Gary, Deputy District Attorney, Contra Costa County, California. Personal Communications.

Kolbuchar, Amy, et al. "Improving Eyewitness Identifications: Hennepin County's Blind Sequential Lineup Pilot Project." Cardozo Public Law, Policy and Ethics Journal, April 2006.

141

Koosed, Margery Malkin. "The Proposed Innocence Protection Act Won't—Unless It Also Curbs Mistaken Eyewitness Identifications." Ohio State Law Journal, 2002.

Krakora, Joseph, Assistant Public Defender for New Jersey. Personal Communications.

Lefstein. "Reform of Defense Representation in Capital Cases: The Indiana Experience and Its Implications for the Nation." Indiana Law Review, 1996.

Lesman. "State Responses to the Specter of Racial Discrimination in Capital Proceedings: The Kentucky Racial Justice Act and the New Jersey Supreme Court's Proportionality Review Project." Journal of Law and Policy, vol. 13, no. 1, 2005.

Liebman, James, et al. "Technical Errors Can Kill." National Law Journal, September 4, 2000.

Liebman. "Opting for Real Death Penalty Reform." Ohio State Law Journal, 2002.

Liptak, Adam. "Maryland Capital Verdicts Show Bias." Crime Control Digest, vol. 37, no. 2, January 17, 2004.

---. NAACP Legal Defense Fund, Death Row, U.S.A., January 1994.

---. "Suspension of Executions is Urged for Pennsylvania." New York Times, March 5, 2003.

Logan. "When Balance and Fairness Collide: An Argument for Execution Impact Evidence in Capital Trials." University of Michigan Journal of Law Reform, 2000.

Lynch, Mona and Haney, Craig. "Discrimination and Instructional Comprehension: Guided Discretion, Racial Bias, and the Death Penalty." Law and Human Behavior, vol. 24, no. 3, June 2000.

Maimonides, Moses. *Mishneh Torah*, Edut.

"Mandatory Justice: Eighteen Reforms to the Death Penalty," Constitution Project, 2001.

Masters, Brooke A. "Missteps on Road to Injustice." *The Washington Post*, December 1, 2000.

Mecklenburg, Sheri, et al. "The Illinois Field Study: A Significant Contribution to Understanding Real World Eyewitness Identification Issues." Law and Human Behavior, February 2008.

Mills, Steve, et al. "Flawed Trials Lead to Death Chamber; Bush Confident in System Rife with Problems." Part 1 of 2, *Chicago Tribune*, June 11, 2000.

"More Death Penalty Doubts." *USA Today*, July 5, 2001 (editorial).

Nagel, Yehoshua. Personal interview. December 22, 2019.

Natarajan, Radha. "Racialized Memory and Reliability: Due Process Applied to Cross-Racial Eyewitness Identifications." New York University Law Review, November 2003.

"No More Excuses. Go to the Tape." *Chicago Tribune*, April 21, 2002.

O'Brien, Tim. "Reasonable Doubt and DNA." *The Washington Post*, September 7, 2000.

Parker, Joshua, Attorney, New York. Personal Communications.

Payne v. Tennessee, 501 U.S. 808 (1991).

Philip, Hager. "Informant Was Coached, Harris Attorneys Say." *Los Angeles Times*, December 1, 1990.

Phillips, Amy. "Thou Shall Not Kill Any Nice People: The Problem of Victim Impact Statements in Capital Sentencing." The American Criminal Law Review, vol. 35, no. 1, Fall 1997.

Platz, Stephanie J. and Harmon M. Hosch. "Cross Racial/Ethnic Eyewitness Identification: A Field Study." Journal of Applied Social Psychology, vol. 18, no. 11, 1988.

Police Executive Research Forum. "A National Survey of Eyewitness Identification Procedures in Law Enforcement Agencies," Research Report Submitted to US Department of Justice, June 1, 2014.

"Police and Pre-Trial Investigations: Chapter 2." Illinois Commission on Capital Punishment, April 15, 2002.

Polish, Dan. "Capital Punishment on Trial: Does Judaism Condone Capital Punishment?" *The Workmen's Circle*. https://circle.org/jsource/capital-punishment-on-trial-does-judaism-condone-capital-punishment-by-rabbi-dan-polish/, accessed on December 23, 2019.

"Pretrial Proceedings: Chapter 8." Illinois Commission on Capital Punishment, April 15, 2002.

"Prosecutors' Selection of Cases for Capital Punishment: Chapter 5." Illinois Commission on Capital Punishment, Final Report, April 15, 2002.

"Protecting the Innocent: Proposals to Reform the Death Penalty." Hearing Before the Committee on the Judiciary, United States Senate.

Public Act 093-0605 and SB 472, Senate Bill from the Illinois State Senate, 2003.

"The Reform of Federal Habeas Corpus in Capital Cases." Duquesne Law Review, 1990.

"Returning to the System's Original Purpose." The Journal of Criminal Law and Criminology, vol. 94, no. 2, winter 2004.

Richardson, John. "Reforming the Jury Override: Protecting Capital Defendants' Rights by Returning to the System's Original Purpose." The Journal of Criminal Law and Criminology, vol. 94, no 2, 2004.

Rosenberg, Benjamin E. "Rethinking the Right to Due Process in Connection with Pretrial Identification Procedures: An Analysis and a Proposal." 79 KY. L. J.,1991.

SB 82, Senate Bill from the West Virginia State Senate, 2007.

Scheck, Barry. "Mistaken Eyewitness Identification: Three Roads to Reform." Champion, National Association of Criminal Defense Lawyers, December 2004.

Shank. "The Death Penalty in Ohio: Fairness, Reliability, and Justice at Risk—A Report on Reforms in Ohio's Use of the Death Penalty Since the 1997 Ohio State Bar Association Recommendations Were Made." Ohio State Law Journal, 2002.

Sharp, Susan F. "Hidden Victims: The Effects of the Death Penalty on Families of the Accused (Critical Issues in Crime and Society)." Rutgers University Press, 2005.

Simon, Jonathan and Christine Spaulding. "Tokens of Our Esteem: Aggravating Factors in the Era of Deregulated Death Penalties." Austin Sarat edition of The Killing State: Capital Punishment in Law Politic and Culture, 1999.

Smolowe, Jill. "Untrue confessions," *Time*, vol.145, no. 21, May 22, 1995.

Solomon, Akiba. "A Matter of Life and Death." *Essence*, vol. 37, no. 1, May 2006.

Sorensen, Jon and Donald Wallace. "Prosecutorial Discretion in Seeking Death: An Analysis of Racial Disparity in the Pretrial Stages of Case Processing in a Midwestern County." Justice Quarterly, vol. 16, no. 3, September 1999.

Steblay, Nancy K. Mehrkens. "Reforming Eyewitness Identification: Cautionary Lineup Instructions; Weighing the Advantages and Disadvantages of Show-

Ups Versus Lineups." Cardozo Public Law, Policy and Ethics Journal, April 2006.

Steele, Lisa. "Trying Identification Cases: An Outline for Raising Eyewitness ID Issues." *The Champion*, November 2004.

Steiker, C., et al. "The Shadow of Death: The Effect of Capital Punishment on American Criminal Law and Policy." *Judicature*, vol. 89, no. 5, March/April 2006.

Stoots-Fonberg, Chasity Anne. "Misguided Instructions: Do Jurors Accurately Understand the Law in Death Penalty Trials?" East Tennessee State University, 2003.

Sullivan, Thomas. "Capital Punishment Reform: What's Been Done and What Remains to Be Done." *The Federal Lawyer*, vol. 51, no. 6, July 2004.

Swarns, Christina. "The Uneven Scales of Capital Justice." *The American Prospect*, vol. 15, no. 7, July 2004.

"Symposium on the death penalty: reforming a process fraught with error." Hofstra Law Review, 2001.

"Symposium: Addressing Capital Punishment Through Statutory Reform." Ohio State Law Journal, 2002.

"Systematic flaws in our criminal justice system." *Judicature* 89, No 5, March 2006.

Tabak, Ronald. "Racial Discrimination in Implementing the Death Penalty." Human Rights, vol. 26, no. 3, Summer 1999.

"Task Force Recommendations on Eyewitness Identification." Prosecutor, National District Attorneys Association, March/April 2005.

Taylor, Stuart, Jr. "For the Record." *American Lawyer*, October 1995.

TerBeek, Calvin. "A Call for Precedential Heads: Why the Supreme Court's Eyewitness Identification Jurisprudence is Anachronistic and Out-of-Step with the Empirical Reality." Law and Psychology Review, Spring 2007.

Tharp, Robert. "Officials Look to Increase Jury Turnout with Proposed Raise." *Knight Ridder Tribune Business News*, May 24, 2005.

Thompson, Jennifer. "I Was Certain, but I Was Wrong." *New York Times*, June 18, 2000.

Thompson-Cannino, Jennifer and Ronald Cotton and Erin Torneo. *Picking Cotton: Our Memoir of Injustice and Redemption*, St. Martin's Press, 2009.

Vreeland, Albert L. II. "The Breath of the Unfee'd Lawyer: Statutory Fee Limitations and Ineffective Assistance of Counsel in Capital Litigation." Michigan Law Review, vol. 90, 1991.

Walker, R. N. "How the Malfunctioning Death Penalty Challenges the Criminal Justice System." *Judicature*.

Warden, Rob. "Illinois Death Penalty Reform: How it Happened, What it Promises." The Journal of Criminal Law and Criminology, vol 85, no. 2, Winter 2005.

Weiers. "The Innocence Protection Act: A Revised Proposal for Capital Punishment Reform." New York University Law of Legislation and Public Policy, vol. 6, no. 2, 2003–2004.

Well, Gary L. and E. P. Seelau. "Eyewitness Identification: Psychological Research and Legal Policy on Lineups." Psychology, Public Policy, and Law, vol. 1, 1995.

Wells, Gary L. "Eyewitness Identification: Systemic Reforms." Wisconsin Law Review, 2006.

---. "Eyewitness Identification Evidence: Science and Reform." Champion, National Association of Criminal Defense Lawyers, April 2005.

---. "Field Experiments on Eyewitness Identification: Towards a Better Understanding of Pitfalls and Prospects." Law and Human Behavior, February 2008.

Wermiel, Stephen. "Supreme Court's Conservative Majority Again Stumbles on Victims-Rights Issue." *Wall Street Journal*, New York, N.Y, Feb 25, 1991.

West Virginia Code § 62-1E

Wiener, R. L. "Death Penalty Research in Nebraska: How Do Judges and Juries Reach Penalty Decisions?" Nebraska Law Review, 2002.

Wood, Jennifer. "Balancing Innocence and Guilt: A Metaphorical Analysis of the US Supreme Court's Rulings on Victim Impact Statements." Western Journal of Communication, vol 69, no. 2, April 2005.

Zanzini, John and Brownlow Speer. "Eye-Witness Identification After Commonwealth v. Martin: Two Views." Boston Bar Journal, January 2007.

Zimring, F. E. "The Unexamined Death Penalty: Capital Punishment and Reform of the Model Penal Code." Columbia Law Review, vol. 105, no. 4, May 2005.

Acknowledgments

I cannot thank enough the individuals who helped bring to publication this book, which originated as my Princeton University senior thesis submitted at the Woodrow Wilson School of Public and International Affairs.

Josh Parker reviewed the draft over a decade ago, prior to its academic submission, and made a number of useful suggestions. The same can be said for Professor Stanley Katz, my advisor at the time. More recently, Yair Manas helped with the review of the current state of case law and social sciences research that have come out since the original drafting. My editor, Sara Pack, has spent countless hours since late 2018 and throughout 2019 assisting with the citations, text standardization, and other necessary steps preparing the book for publication. Finally, I would like to thank my wife, Rivkah Spolin, for providing support and insight through the process.

Index

Made in the USA
Middletown, DE
19 February 2020